About Demos

Demos is a greenhouse for new ideas which can improve the quality of our lives. As an independent think tank, we aim to create an open resource of knowledge and learning that operates beyond traditional party politics.

We connect researchers, thinkers and practitioners to an international network of people changing politics. Our ideas regularly influence government policy, but we also work with companies, NGOs, colleges and professional bodies.

Demos knowledge is organised around five themes, which combine to create new perspectives. The themes are democracy, learning, enterprise, quality of life and global change.

But we also understand that thinking by itself is not enough. Demos has helped to initiate a number of practical projects which are delivering real social benefit through the redesign of public services.

We bring together people from a wide range of backgrounds to cross-fertilise ideas and experience. By working with Demos, our partners develop a sharper insight into the way ideas shape society. For Demos, the process is as important as the final product.

www.demos.co.uk

First published in 2004

ISBN 1 84180 129 1
Typeset by Land & Unwin, Bugbrooke
Printed by Hendy Banks, London

For further information and
subscription details please contact:

Demos
Magdalen House
136 Tooley Street
London SE1 2TU

telephone: 0845 458 5949
email: hello@demos.co.uk
web: www.demos.co.uk

Eternal Youths

How the baby boomers are having their time again

James Harkin
Julia Huber

DEMOS

Contents

Acknowledgements

We are very grateful to Centrica and Saga Group for supporting this project. Special thanks are owed to Kevin Doyle and Andrew McCallum from Centrica and Tim Bull, Torben Jessen and John Pickett from Saga Group for their contributions throughout the research process.

We benefited greatly from our conversations with a number of experts who shared their knowledge and ideas with us. Thanks to Tamar Kasriel, Richard Tomkins, Thomas Endres, Susan Hewer, Professor Jeremy Myerson, Dr George Leeson, Robert Brown and Guy Robinson, Dr David Metz, Daniel Howse and all those who participated in the Demos seminar.

For the case studies we are much indebted to Susan Snyder, Lorian Coutts, Louise Parkes, Lucy Shadbolt, Foeke de Jong and Michelle Sohn.

We would like to particularly thank Alison Percy and Fiona Gillard for their help with the focus groups, and Jane Robinson for her help with the MORI data.

We are especially grateful to Cheryl Kernot for her comments and advice on the research process and several drafts of this report.

At Demos, Rachel McLachlan provided invaluable support in the development stage and at crucial points throughout the project. Sarah Gillinson provided very able research assistance in the initial phase of the project and Adam White helped with the case studies and events.

Thanks also to Bobby Webster and Eddie Gibb. Finally, our thanks to Tom Bentley for his guidance and inspiration when it was most needed.

All of these people and many more made invaluable contributions; as usual though, any omissions and errors remain our own.

James Harkin
Julia Huber
June 2004

Foreword

In 1991, British Gas, in collaboration with Help the Aged, commissioned a report entitled 'Attitudes to Ageing', which highlighted the issues facing older people and contributed to our understanding of their needs in a changing society.

Thirteen years on, society continues to change, but Centrica remains deeply committed to this important issue through our partnership with Demos. In this report, we look at the service needs of an older society.

At Centrica, we believe that our continued success will depend on deepening our relationships with customers. But this will only be achieved by working to understand their needs, both now and in the future.

This report highlights that older consumers will increasingly look to trusted organisations to make their lives easier by acting as 'gatekeepers', managing a range of products and services. At Centrica, we aim to be the customers' first choice through our well-known and trusted brands, led by British Gas.

This report challenges the private, public and charitable sectors to look at new and innovative ways of providing services in a future society where older people are in the majority. Centrica, already at the forefront of community initiatives, intends to heed this call. We will continue to develop new strategies and partnerships such that we can meet the needs of all our stakeholders in a responsible way.

Centrica recognises that an ageing UK demographic will have an impact, not only on the marketplace, but also in the workplace. We are already looking at the implications of an ageing workforce as part of our overall diversity strategy because we recognise that an ageing and increasingly diverse society will be best served by a diverse and inclusive organisation.

Centrica is pleased to be associated with this Demos report and the contribution it makes to this important debate.

Sir Roy Gardner, chief executive, Centrica

1. Introduction

'The baby boomers are coming!' shouted the 2003 newspaper headline.

While the 'ageing society' – and tabloid hyberbole about a 'demographic time-bomb' – springs from the realisation that we are living longer than ever before, it is only quite recently that public debate connected this increase in longevity with the very specific cohort of people now limbering up for older life. This is the unusual demographic blip of babies born in the UK between 1945 and 1965. This group is now aged between 39 and 59, and contemplating what it will be like to pass through the turnstile into old age.

The baby boomers have always been seen as a deeply symbolic generation – swollen by a surge of postwar optimism, reaching adulthood in tandem with the 1960s and a new set of social freedoms, consumer innovations and political conflicts. For many of them, challenging received wisdom is deeply embedded in their own self-image. As they age, we should not expect this characteristic to be diminished.

The age structure of the British population is in a state of flux. According to the statisticians, there were 19.6 million people aged over 50 in Britain in the year 2000. In 2010 the figure will be 21.9 million and by 2025 it will be 26.7 million.[1] According to figures produced by the Employers Forum on Age (EFA), the number of people in the UK aged between 16 and 50 will fall by 1.5 million over the next quarter-century, while the number of those aged 50 and above will rise by more than 6 million.[2]

The number of British baby boomers is enough to warrant the attention of social scientists and policy-makers. But they also appear to have distinctive values. In 2003, *The New Old*, published by Demos, sparked widespread debate about how the attitudes and values of British boomers might be channelled into improving everyone's quality of life at the beginning of the twenty-first century.[3] But one problem in thinking about British baby boomers is that very little original research has addressed them directly. Only in the last couple of years, as baby boomers have arrived at the apex of the generational spectrum, have organisations begun to think seriously about how to adapt their services, offerings and communication accordingly. Only in the United States, where the baby boomers are much more vocal in the articulation of their interests, has there been sustained research into their values.

This report takes on the challenge of exploring directly the hopes, fears, perceptions and priorities of a group of British men and women who may help to reshape the meaning of 'old age', and will play a pivotal role in negotiating the wider social and economic transitions that Britain also faces. In talking directly to baby boomers, we have tested assumptions about how age, sex, marital status and ethnicity impact on the values of British baby boomers.

Some firms are already waking up to the fact that, while youth culture might be 'cool', it is far cooler to profit from the well-heeled baby boomers. Current estimates suggest that over-45s in the UK are now responsible for nearly 80 per cent of all financial wealth, and are responsible for 30 per cent of all consumer spending.[4] But as the baby boomers continue to march through the life cycle in huge numbers, our conclusion is that the financial clout they wield will be less important than the novel ways in which they will want to spend their money – and what they will expect in return.

Our research uncovers three core themes and issues that demand greater attention from those seeking to provide services, win votes or attract loyalty and commitment from baby boomers in the years ahead. They are likely to show up on the political radar eventually, but perhaps more importantly they will help to change the way that many of our everyday institutions, from banking to healthcare, are organised and delivered.

Living life again

Many baby boomers are beginning to enjoy a windfall; the combination of wealth, health and longer life gives them a new phase of life. In this phase they have the chance to 'live again', to focus on being mature but independent, discerning but carefree, and in which they can revisit their own desire for personal fulfilment free from the pressures of overwork and childrearing.

For those who can afford it, a new 'experience economy' of travel, food, learning and lifestyle is growing rapidly. Baby boomers used to working full time are preoccupied with re-establishing sovereignty over their own routines, and with making use of flexibility to enjoy themselves. Those who find themselves single speak warmly about their ability to enjoy active sex lives. Those released from decades of full-time work are hungrily searching out new cultural and consumption experiences.

In doing so, and prolonging the active, healthy and independent stage of older life, baby boomers will increasingly be looking to support and service organisations for help. The people we talked to strongly defended the principles of welfare and free healthcare, and wanted guarantees of support and security. But increasingly, they see these fixed points, including retirement income and assets, as a bulwark against which they can experiment with more flexible ways of living. Baby boomers will be increasingly interested in new forms of part-time work and income if they feel that they can maintain them on their own terms. If they feel they are being manipulated or having the rules changed, they are likely to rebel vociferously.

Colonising popular culture

As a generation, the baby boomers are likely to reject many of the traditional associations of old age. In making personal fulfilment after

50 their priority, the research shows that many will use their purchasing power, connections and self-awareness increasingly to dominate the images and rituals of popular culture. From middle-aged men and women on motorbikes to new beauty products and treatments and music retailing, the dominance of baby boomers and their own formative icons will only grow.

Though much media and marketing are now criticised for their obsession with youth as the key, trend-setting demographic, it is less well understood that the baby boomers will have little trouble in reaching for aspects of youth culture which appeal to them. As a result, cultures and social movements that are distinctively 'young' may be increasingly difficult to find, and the effects on younger generations' own self-image and rituals of identity are impossible to predict.

A good death

In many respects, infirmity and death are the great unspoken shadow looming behind the confidence and power of the baby boomers. While they are open, reflective and comfortable with their own sense of personal identity, much of their energy (and cash) seem to flow into things which help to preserve a sense of youth and vitality. During the project many talked about their fear of dependence and isolation, and their concern with quality of life as well as with prolonging it is palpable.

The evidence appears to show that far fewer baby boomers than previous generations are concerned with passing inheritance on to their children, but that they are equally preoccupied with not becoming 'a burden'. Many, for example, appear ready and willing to pay for long-term care rather than stifling the lives of their children.

And while the fitness, wellness and personal support sectors may well thrive in response to these priorities in the coming decades, it is inevitable that, as they age, a critical mass of baby boomers will confront questions of death and dying more explicitly.

Much of the health and long-term care debate in the UK so far has been about the projected costs of provision, but these changing priorities surely also signal a coming debate about the manner of provision. Just as baby boomers have sought to customise their living experiences, so they will also begin to demand a greater say in the management and timing of their own deaths. Our research uncovered the way in which funerals and death ceremonies are becoming increasingly personalised. More open, explicit and politically mainstream debates about the nature of death and the transition towards it will follow sooner rather than later. This includes euthanasia and assisted deaths, the nature of palliative and hospice care and their costs, and a host of related issues.

These themes help us to build a picture of the priorities and preconceptions that stand behind the social and lifestyle changes already going on among the baby boomer generation. It is through these millions of personal adjustments that the social and institutional contours of British life will also adapt over the next generation. A host of more detailed issues will also play an important part, from political activism to technology use, whom the baby boomers trust to whether they can care for their own parents. But the centre of gravity is shifting towards a cohort intent on rediscovering 'middle youth' after middle age, and we would do well to understand that self-perception more accurately.

The research process

To stimulate our research process, Demos began by interviewing a variety of different experts in the field. In addition to interviewing experts and interested parties, the research process for this report included eight group discussions with British baby boomers as well as a series of case studies.

Sessions for the focus groups were conducted in London, Leeds, Bradford and Dorset. Each session lasted approximately two hours and comprised six to eight respondents. Participants were selected in a manner sensitive to their age, ethnic group, sex and income bracket. The sample was divided as follows:

- Group 1: 40–50-year-olds, AB(C1), London

- Group 2: 40–50-year-olds, C2DE, London
- Group 3: 40–50-year-olds, C1C2, Asian (Muslim) women, Bradford
- Group 4: 40–50-year-olds, AB(C1), Dorset
- Group 5: 50–60-year-olds, C2DE, Dorset
- Group 6: 50–60-year-olds, C1C2, African-Caribbean, London
- Group 7: 50–60-year-olds, C1C2, London
- Group 8: 50–60-year-olds, (A)BC1, Leeds

There are, it must be remembered, clear limitations to any process of qualitative research, and the primary research referred to in the following report is based on a relatively small sample of interviewees. Nonetheless, our research revealed strong and consistent messages about the preoccupations and preferences of baby boomers. We are confident that these can be generalised across a much broader sample.

2. Paradoxes of middle youth

a portrait of the baby boomer at mid-life

How old is old? What it means to grow old is surely dependent on context and the society in which you live. But it also depends on where you are standing, on how old you are. Throughout the course of our research with baby boomers, the most illuminating touchstone of their values was in their approaches to old age and death. In short, they had nothing but scorn for the idea that they might be considered as old.

> *When you are younger you think middle age is old but when you get there you think it is young.*
>
> *The more you enjoy yourself, the younger you feel.*
>
> *I still feel 18.*

Staying young in appearance was considered vitally important for many of our interviewees. Taking care over one's appearance was felt by women to indicate an inner state of mind: continuing to put effort into one's appearance was a sign of continuing to engage with the world and of maintaining a sense of dignity and self-respect. For the boomers we interviewed, the need to remain beautiful was less about being young than preserving the status quo against the ravages of age.

> *When I was 20 I thought 50 was old and that is what all my relatives acted like because at 50 you were old but I think our*

generation doesn't act like that. On the inside I feel 23 and my daughter is now older than I am!

I am scared of getting old but I feel if I keep going I can delay it. Do what you have always done until you drop basically.

I have started to wear make-up now that makes me look like I am not wearing make-up because I don't want to look like mutton dressed as lamb.

If many of our interviewees seemed determined to retain their youthful looks, they considered that they had good reasons for so doing. To them, the idea of being old carried connotations not only of uselessness and decrepitude but also of the guilt of being a social burden. The baby boomers we interviewed were keen to articulate their frustration with contemporary media representations of old people, the practical result of hysterical media coverage about the so-called 'demographic time-bomb':

The newspapers are always saying that we are a burden on the young. There is a deep attitude problem.

At the same time, however, some were proud to celebrate the internal or mental advantages which they had accrued from growing older, chiefly, experience and wisdom:

Having experience of things, so you know how to react to a certain situation and perhaps you can counsel your kids a bit. Having a better perspective, I suppose.

The freedom to do

The fact that we can expect to live longer than our ancestors is part of our debt to modern society and the modern infrastructure, technology and medicine which help to keep us alive. But our ideas about ageing are also socially constructed, and depend on broader social and cultural understandings of what it is to grow old. The fact that some of us still believe that old age begins at 65 stems from the postwar origins of the modern welfare state, and society's calculations at that time about when it could afford to have us retire.[5] Our conversations with baby boomers suggest that this is a construction whose time has passed, and which needs to be renewed in a different form. Many of those baby boomers felt that old age began at 80, a full 15 years beyond our traditional state pension age.

> *Ten years ago someone of 65 was retired and that was it, but now . . . they are in B&Q.*
>
> *Why are older people more keen to work for us? A combination of financial necessity and the wish not to get bored out of your brain.*
>
> Interview with Lorian Coutts,
> Director of Communications, B&Q

Our baby boomers were determined not to be forced to retire, and felt that they might have many fruitful and productive years ahead of them. Most workers, especially the professionals among them, saw work an essential part of their life, and one which they would not want automatic retirement from at the age of 65.

> *Yes, I like working. I feel that if you are working with younger people it keeps you young as well.*

> *I think it should be possible to work when you are older if you want to.*

> *There is a desire to keep on working; my father is 82 and retired at the basic age of 65. He was a college lecturer and when he retired his brain just was not able to keep going, and he just basically almost became senile overnight. He is not senile but he slowed down so quickly and I wouldn't like to see myself as being a gardener at 65.*

> *I think the saddest thing is being sat at home doing absolutely nothing.*

At the same time, they were suspicious of any government which might coerce them to work beyond their formal retirement age, and withhold pension entitlements as an incentive.

> *You should not be made to feel you are beholden to them. If you have worked all your life you have put into the health service, privately or whatever, then you should be reaping the benefits because when you get older is when you need it. They should understand that.*

What was important for baby boomers was to win a guarantee that their existing social entitlements were protected, and to use that as a springboard to be creative about their plans in their third age. Perhaps most importantly, the boomers did not want to be dictated to by authorities or those in power. The desire of baby boomers to 'do it themselves', their refusal to be dictated to by anyone, was well illustrated in their approach to work.

> *I want to do more of my own stuff which obviously I wouldn't get paid for . . . I might be working for myself and getting no remuneration out of it at all but I would get pleasure out of it.*

The most common value associated with the baby boomers that we interviewed was freedom.

> *We wouldn't want to be told what to do.*

> *Just complete freedom.*

> *Time to do things and time for yourself.*

> *Easier pace of life really.*

> *I would still be drinking coffee, going out for a cappuccino every now and again. Visiting art galleries, which I like doing, gardening and cooking with family. Eating nice food. I have actually got a mobile home by the sea now anyway but I would like to branch further afield, maybe see more of the world.*

Our baby boomer interviewees saw retirement as more of a time for adventure and exploration, even wanting to imitate the 'gap year' teenager in travelling to unusual places, meeting local people and discovering other ways of life.

To have a holiday home abroad.

This [picture from his collage] is just a guy lying down and relaxing and I would like to think in 20 years' time I will be able to chill out and do what I want when I want.

Travelling, hopefully I will still be mobile enough to enjoy travelling.

In essence, many of our baby boomers were looking forward to a life which consisted simply of them and their partner, where they could spend time cooking a lovely meal for two rather than churning out vast quantities of food for all the family. They envisaged less stress, less rushing around, the opportunity to put their feet up – time that was filled neither with work nor with their children. While this is certainly an articulation of an ideal, and many, when prompted, accepted that in reality this probably wouldn't come about, the hope for simplicity and slowing down of time which it reveals is genuine. This is worth bearing in mind when considering the tone and content of any communication with this age group.

As they moved towards old age, our baby boomers also maintained that they would have the freedom to take risks – in everything from what they wore to the career path that they followed – and expected to be recognised and rewarded for doing so. Some of our older baby boomers, those in their 50s, had already taken unconventional or risky career choices – setting up their own business later in life, for example – and enthused about the emotional and financial rewards of so doing. They did not appear to feel greatly constrained by pressure from, or expectations of, those around them.

We are more versatile, more adaptable [than previous generations].

Many felt that they were allowed to be individuals and to express their individual personalities in potentially quirky or unorthodox ways; women who were divorced or separated, for example, were clearly enjoying the sexual freedom this presented them with. Our younger boomer interviewees, now in their 40s, were often positive about getting older and determined to see it as an opportunity – to travel, to learn new things, to keep fit, able and busy in their older age. They expected to grow old in a different way from their parents, eg by still wearing the clothes they do now ('combats and trainers') and still doing the things they do now ('going for a cappuccino'). They refused to be constrained by expectations of 'appropriate behaviour'.

Baby boomers' insistence on the need for an active and creative retirement combined with their reluctance to be coerced into working longer has strong implications for policy-making. In the first place, it suggests that a government intent on encouraging the next generation of older people to work beyond 65 should focus on offering 'carrots' rather than 'sticks' – positive incentives which encourage older people to continue working rather than negative incentives which penalise them for refusing to work.[6] Thus raising the mandatory retirement age to 70 is likely to be less appealing to baby boomers than abolishing it altogether.

More generally, however, and beyond the remit of any specific legislation, it suggests how we might begin to reinvent the whole idea of retirement for the twenty-first century. Our baby boomer interviewees refused to see retirement as an ending. Rather than a linear progression through a series of discrete stages, they preferred to see their life as a fluid cycle, one which would enable them to dip in and out of periods of education, work and active leisure as and when they saw fit. A society that wants to continue to benefit from the creativity and continued labour of its ageing population needs to think about making radical changes to its employment and taxation policies to give ageing citizens as much freedom as they need.

Don't mind the gap

The desire among baby boomers to hold on to their youth is not just about warding off the outer manifestations of physical decline. Increasingly, their relationships with their children are relationships among equals. A recent poll of 1,219 American parents by RoperASW is nicely illustrative of this lack of a generation gap. As many as one in ten American parents of children under 18, the poll concluded, said they had smoked marijuana in the preceding 12 months; one in 20, or about 3 million people, said they had smoked in the preceding month. Years after battles with their own parents over drug use, it seems, many baby boomers are facing the thorny issue of how to reconcile their use of soft drugs with their parental responsibilities. Many of those same parents, according to a report in the *New York Times*, have now been reduced to concealing furtive puffs from children whose views on drugs are much more conservative. 'I go to great lengths,' a New York professional with two pre-teenage children told the *New York Times* reporter. 'I put towels under the door, I use baby powder to hide the smell. If I say I'm going to Costco, my babysitter knows.'[7]

Tempting as it was, our research among British baby boomers did not enquire into their drug habits. Nevertheless, it seemed significant that our interviewees tended to characterise the relationship between themselves and their children as one of equals, and certainly more equal than the relationship which they had once enjoyed with their own parents.

> *I would not say I feel 41, you look at the kids, I sometimes think we mess around the same as what they do, you do not act your age, not like my parents used to.*

> *Our kids will discuss things with us that I would not even dream of talking to my mother about.*

The exception to this was among our minority ethnic participants – even the younger minority ethnic participants – where most within the groups insisted on the essential difference between children and their parents.

They've got to know their rights and wrongs. You have to be strict at times, I think.

Fear and loathing of old age

In general, however, our respondents were often reluctant to engage with being older. It was not only that they struggled to think about what the future might be like. More importantly, they struggled to imagine the prospect of their own future, and how their third age might turn out. They were terrified of the physiological changes which are irreversible and which accompany old age:

I just don't want to think that far ahead.

My greatest fear is: how am I going to die?

Sixteen years ago I was only 28. But in 16 years' time I'll be 60.

Those worries about ageing were exacerbated by the way in which old people are marginalised.

I'm worried about being on the scrapheap.

Some, however, were more resigned:

It's like the tide, you can't hold it back.

That is not something that worries me, if my number is up my number is up.

There was good evidence that the boomers are, true to stereotype, indeed an 'idealistic' generation. Respondents, for example, were required to construct a collage of how they saw their lives in 20 or so years' time. Although asked to think about their future in terms that were as *realistic* as possible, the majority created an *ideal* or included an element of their 'ideal'. When pushed, it was clear that many were fearful of 'getting old' and all the attendant associations of physical and mental degeneration that that suggested. There was general agreement that, whereas someone in their 60s used to be regarded as elderly, it would be possible for *them* to be 60-something and still behave and feel much as they do now. Most considered that old age would arrive when they reached 80 years of age. Until that time they hoped to remain mentally active. Maintaining one's physical well-being was thought essential to putting off the onset of old age. Many were adamant in their refusal to be sent out to pasture:

> *I don't want to be like a real old lady, I want to be active.*
>
> *I don't think we'll be doing sedentary type things like bowling, I think we'll be doing more active things.*
>
> *I go to the gym now and I want to stay healthy like I am and I don't want to be like old women who don't bother about their health.*
>
> *I pump myself up with many vitamins. Even though I try not to think about it, you have to start looking after yourself now.*
>
> *Keep taking the pills . . . vitamins.*

Hardly surprisingly, however, being 'old old', the age which our interviewees tended to think began at the age of 80, carried a large number of very negative associations.

> *Old old, as far as I can see to be perfectly honest, there's not a lot to look forward to.*

Among our interviewees, there was a clear dislike of the physical signs of ageing – especially among women, who talked about their fears of wrinkly skin and grey hair, and often expressed horror that they were already experiencing some of these signs. The possibility of senility also raised a chill, as did thoughts of illness and protracted pain or suffering. People talked about becoming 'trapped' by their physical dependence on others, and their desire to avoid becoming a burden was very strong. There was also a genuine fear of becoming somehow sidelined or redundant, of being put on the shelf and left to grow old. All in all, becoming 'old old' presented a pretty miserable scenario to most. Much of the discussion of people's hopes and needs for when they were 'older' tended to focus on the period between 'retirement' and the time when they would be too frail to do what they wanted or to live independently. This middle period could be viewed positively, even looked forward to, whereas the feeling was that once the 'old old' stage had been reached, there was little that they could do to affect their quality of life.

All this is not entirely new. Recent research from experts at the respected Fondation Nationale de Gérontologie (FNG) in France, for example, has shown that French baby boomers find it difficult if not impossible to conceive of someone more elderly as representing their own future. To counteract the horror of ageing among the middle-aged in France, French gerontologists are working with children to change society's bleak perception of the ageing process. Since middle-aged French people are so afraid of growing old that they are in denial, the researchers decided that their awareness programme would have to leapfrog a generation in order to effect any change.[8] Elsewhere, some epidemiologists are now arguing that fears about growing old might even precipitate an early death. In September 2002, Becca R Levy, an epidemiologist at Yale University, warned a US Senate Special Committee on Aging that 'extolling youthfulness while demeaning the old helps to generate images that may have devastating consequences.' Levy had just completed a 20-year study, published in the *Journal of Personality and Social Psychology*, which discovered that older individuals with more positive self-perceptions of ageing, measured up to 23 years earlier, lived 7.5 years longer than those with less positive self-perceptions of ageing.[9]

Policy-making, however, is too blunt an instrument to deal with the fear and loathing which seem to degrade the idea of growing old in the minds of many baby boomers. That can only be solved by a culture shift. It is a paradox of our ageing society that many of us seem increasingly obsessed with the idea of youth. If baby boomers are to be at ease with themselves, we conclude, they need to fortify themselves with a story about the benefits of ageing. Rather than regressing to its youth, our ageing society might do well to reclaim some of the benefits of growing older: wisdom, finesse and accumulated experience.

On similar lines the German commentator and intellectual Frank Schirrmacher, one of the publishers of the *Frankfurter Allgemeine Zeitung*, recently argued in his best-selling book *Das Methusalem Komplott* (*The Methuselah Conspiracy*) for a fundamental cultural change in our perceptions of ageing if we wanted to make the transition to an ageing society a positive experience. Schirrmacher calls for a 'conspiracy' between future generations of older people against our obsession with youth culture and the 'biological and social terror' generated by the pervasive age discrimination that currently dominates our society.[10]

The 'little blue pill' of euthanasia

The discussion of 'death' as an inevitable part of growing old was avoided in the group sessions – often until the point when it could be avoided no longer. Respondents were generally uncomfortable about the issue at first, but relieved once it had been brought up, and often warmed to the topic. A handful were more matter-of-fact about the matter, declaring that they expected not to be around in, say, 20 years' time; some talked about ill health running in their family and this affected their expectations for their own lifespan.

For most, the biggest concern around death was the idea of 'lingering', of growing ill or frail and increasingly unable to care for themselves mentally or physically. The ideal was a 'quick death' allowing them to maintain their self-respect. They wanted to go peacefully, in their own home, while they were enjoying life and before they had become dependent on others. In a number of groups, respondents said their preference would be to take a pill themselves or for someone to kill them before their quality of life became severely affected by frailty or illness. Most wanted to avoid 'being looked after' altogether and hoped to die before this happened. In most groups the rights and wrongs of assisted suicide and euthanasia were debated in both a moral and legal sense. In all of those groups, there was strong support for the right to choose assisted suicide or euthanasia and a feeling that this might offer the best solution for everyone – the elderly person themselves, their family and the state. On the idea of euthanasia, many seemed very positive:

> *I would like to choose to end my life.*
>
> *I hope someone will come in and put a pillow over my head.*
>
> *It fills me with horror, the idea of becoming dependent. I can see the value where it is appropriate and necessary but it is not something I look forward to. That might be the time to take the little blue pill.*
>
> *Euthanasia – I am all for it.*
>
> *If I was terminally ill I would want that.*

There was also a great deal of enthusiasm for other, associated services.

> *I'd like to see it legal then, if you could write a living will and say – if I'm reduced to a vegetative state, then I would like to put an end to my life.*

Many of our interviewees were quite keen to discuss how they might end their own lives.

> *Yes, but if your life is just sitting in a chair watching telly then that is not a life, is it.*
>
> *If your quality of life is at the stage where you don't think it is worth living I think you should have the choice.*
>
> *If I lost my independence then I would rather go.*

Baby boomers' enthusiasm for the principle of euthanasia emphasises the urgent need for an open public debate on the moral and legal questions surrounding euthanasia and assisted suicide. It also suggests that, whatever people say about an ageing society, baby boomers are not motivated by longevity alone: they are interested in quality of life, and are happy to pull the plug if that quality dissipates.

But it also suggests a more general lesson. Since the ability to manage one's death is perhaps the consumer service *par excellence*, the weight which boomers attach to choosing the time of their own exit as well as the manner of that exit is a good indication of the premium that they place on choice. The same goes for their funerals. Determined not to be part of the herd, baby boomers, especially in America but also in this country, are increasingly planning a highly customised and personalised leave-taking – one punctuated by the songs of Led Zeppelin, for example, or leavened by a troupe of dancers. The American writer Joe Queenan has chronicled the way in which wealthy American baby boomers are customising funeral services, 'transforming funerals into a slapdash mixture of performance art, stand-up comedy, and karaoke'.[11] The implications for public, voluntary and private sector organisations are obvious. Baby boomers need to be treated as individuals, and want, wherever possible, the opportunity to customise their own products and services from a broad palette of choices.

3. Consumption, customisation and choice

Consumers, in the words of the American advertising agency executive David Lubars, 'are like roaches – you spray them and spray them and they get immune after a while'.[12] If Lubars is right, then the baby boomers can claim to be the roaches *par excellence*. They were the first ever generation to grow up in the 'mass consumption' society as it emerged in the years after the Second World War. As a result, they are highly experienced consumers who have shaped and been shaped by the demands and expectations of consumer society. But just how have their preferences been shaped as they enter mid-life, and how should those in the advertising and communication industry begin to respond to those changes?

The struggle which many mainstream brands will have to win the attention of this cynical cohort was demonstrated by our qualitative research among baby boomers. Asked to think of examples of communication that appealed to them, many struggled with this to the point where a number of 50–60-year-old respondents – enough to suggest that this is certainly a widespread reaction – brought with them examples, not of communication which they like, but of things which they object to or feel 'bombarded' by. Most common among these were direct mail about financial services (especially credit cards), and newspaper and magazine adverts for mobile phones and financial services.

You see offers this week, in which the store says it's closing on Wednesday. Then next week you see exactly the same offer, and the store is still open.

There is way too much junk mail rubbish.

More generally, our research suggested that a great deal of their residual political radicalism and non-conformism had been sublimated into an uncompromisingly militant approach to their rights as a consumer. In most areas of consumption, but particularly with regard to financial services, the majority of our respondents were keen to label themselves as 'savvy consumers' who would not be 'duped' by clever marketing. Some even went further, identifying themselves as truculent, self-consciously irascible complainants. A common theme that emerged from our interviews with baby boomers themselves was a sense of themselves as a generation of 'whingers' or 'moaners' (the programme *Grumpy Old Men* was often referred to here). When asked to think about a planet solely populated by baby boomers, for example, one of our interviewees labelled it 'Planet Whinger'. Others voiced the reservation that it 'would be full of people moaning all the time'. There was also the pervasive sentiment that they have been let down by institutions they once used to trust, and had every reason to be grumpy.

It's a cultural thing, older people have been through the war and they don't complain so much. But I think customer expectations on the whole are growing. As those baby boomers grow older, I think they will become more vocal. They'll be standing up on telly saying – why isn't this happening? They will be lobbying government.

Interview with Lorian Coutts,
Director of Communications, B&Q

Surveys of British baby boomers have arrived at similar conclusions. In 2002, for example, research from MORI discovered that British baby boomers were angry and frustrated about British life. The survey, published by MORI's Social Research Institute, identified the 'Meldrews' as British people between the ages of 35 and 54. Meldrews, according to MORI, are fed up with the pressures of working long hours, are disillusioned with conventional political parties and are pessimistic about the prospects of improvements in the NHS or public transport. Only 5 per cent of those surveyed thought the NHS would improve, compared with 18 per cent among the under-34s and 19 per cent among the over-55s.[13]

> *Back in the 1960s, I think that they had faith in technology and the idea that they could change the world. But where are the jet-packs now? Nowadays, it seems, they have metamorphosed into grumpy old men, permanently disillusioned by the fact that the future that they looked forward to never happened.*
>
> Richard Tomkins, columnist, *Financial Times*

But the baby boomers are not only disillusioned by services – they are also more assertive than any previous generation in demanding what they take to be their rights. Their assertiveness, will, over the next decade, have profound implications for how many of our public services are organised. The Wanless Report on the future of NHS funding, for example, has already argued that 'it is likely that future older people will be increasingly intolerant of any differential access to services. They are likely to be more demanding of the health service, thanks to greater awareness of health and available interventions.' The report also noted evidence from the Nuffield Trust that the number of complaints by older people was already increasing, and from Age Concern that older adults were becoming increasingly proactive in their requests for screening.[14]

Our research among baby boomers evidenced a great deal of pride in the welfare state in general and the NHS in particular.

> *I do have a lot of trust in the NHS, all of my experiences have been good. And equally so, other institutions such as the education system in this country are very sound generally.*

Nevertheless, a number of our interviewees voiced strong reservations. A number, for example, had had negative experiences – of misdiagnosis or failure to be taken seriously – with their GP. Others were simply concerned about the level of aftercare within the NHS:

> *I wouldn't trust my GP with my life at all. I'd look at an encyclopaedia or surf the internet.*
>
> *The NHS is a black hole, fantastic in an emergency. But there is no aftercare.*

There is also evidence that boomers will make more demanding givers. In a finding which looks likely to have broader implications for marketers and advertisers as well as charitable organisations, American researchers studying the charitable giving trends of different age groups in the US say that baby boomers are changing the business of giving. For example, they rarely respond to requests for donations made on the telephone or in the mail. Instead they seek out charities that reflect their interests and concerns, and then carefully scrutinise the organisations' financial statements. Michael Nilsen, a spokesman for the Association of Fundraising Professionals, recently told the *Associated Press* that 'people born before World War II tend to see charities as authority figures and tend to be a little more reserved.' Baby boomers, by contrast, 'tend to consider themselves more to be equals of charitable leaders and organizations. They like to seek out charities to donate to . . . and they really want to focus on results.' By way of response, many charities in the US are already communicating much more with boomers than previous generations about how money is being spent. They're also making much more use of newsletters, surveys and the internet to keep boomers informed.[15]

The elixir of youth

It is, as we have seen, an enduring paradox of our ageing society that it seems increasingly obsessed with the idea of youth. An Australian government study on population ageing and the economy published in 2001, for example, discovered that while boomers are in general very savvy consumers, they do have an Achilles heel – how they manage their health.[16] The same boomers who pride themselves on their astuteness as consumers, it seems, may be highly credulous about the prospect of buying the elixir of youth. It is already widely accepted that pharmaceutical and cosmetics manufacturers stand to prosper as a result of boomer anxieties about beauty, health and well-being. Global demand for cosmetic anti-ageing products alone, according to a recent report, is set to rocket by around 11 per cent per year to reach US$29 billion in 2007.[17] Astute food manufacturers are busily upgrading their products to add so-called 'functional' or 'nutraceutical' ingredients: ones which help prevent against diseases or which purport to delay the ageing process. Again in the US, gym membership and fitness programmes have also witnessed a boom as the boomers age and have more time both to exercise and to worry about their fitness. Gyms are developing 'second chance' and 'new me' programmes – low-impact classes aimed at an older constituency, including Tai Chi, water aerobics and Pilates.[18] In coming years, the boomers look likely to be a force to be reckoned with in the leisure industry.

British boomers, if our interviewees are to be believed, are quickly catching up with their American cousins. Many of our boomer interviewees were convinced that healthy living is on the increase, and that this is a good thing. They imagine that they will have more free time, more leisure, that they could retire to live abroad. But one of their chief concerns is to mask or defy the outward signs of ageing:

> *I am still looking for the best anti-wrinkle cream going.*
>
> *I don't want to be old and ugly. I'm paranoid about it.*

A minority, however, were unhappy at what they saw as the manipulations of the anti-ageing industry.

> *We are bombarded with anti-ageing products. Now the men are more beautiful than the women.*

The vogue for grooming is not solely a female preoccupation. In our groups, the claimed indifference of men to their appearance may be, to some extent, a research effect, exaggerated by a desire not to appear vain in front of their peers. In 2002, it is worth noting, global sales of men's grooming products reached US$11 billion in 2003, accounting for 15 per cent of the total beauty products market.[19] In America, the ubiquitous futurologist and trend spotter Faith Popcorn has recently argued that male vanity – what she calls 'manity' – will be one of the most important trends of the decade. The phenomenon, she argues, is driven largely by ageing male baby boomers who are defying the ageing process with as much gusto as they refused to conform in the 1960s. Watch out, she says, for the growth of numerous male institutions once reserved for women, such as men's day spas and salons, offering an extensive selection of relaxation and grooming treatments and services specifically for men. Businesses like these, according to Popcorn, are set to become the networking hubs of the future.[20]

Popcorn is not alone in predicting an advancing army of middle-aged Dorian Grays. Michael Weiss, an analyst who writes for *American Demographics* magazine, has identified American middle-class men in their 40s, the last of the postwar baby boomers who grew up in the youth-obsessed 1960s and 1970s, as key drivers of the 'grey beauty' industry. The most expensive purchases tracked by Weiss are hormone injections which offer better skin tone, muscle flexibility and sex drive.[21]

Beyond health and beauty treatments available over the counter or at a leisure centre, the issue of plastic surgery was raised spontaneously in a number of our conversations with baby boomers. In general, our older interviewees were more hostile to the idea of plastic surgery, more prone to regard it as vain and self-indulgent. At the younger end of the age spectrum, however, our interviewees were more accepting of the cosmetic surgeon's knife. A couple of the younger, urban, female respondents were prepared to admit they might consider minor operations to maintain their looks and some claimed to know friends of the same age who had succumbed to such treatments. It was also noteworthy that the role models of their age group identified by our interviewee, particularly the women, all looked good for their age: Cliff Richard, Liz Taylor, Joanna Lumley, Felicity Kendall. Many were struggling with the idea of whether nature can be improved upon, attempting to redraw a line in the sand. But our research offers some support for the fact that 'plastic surgery' has 'tipped' in the imagination of British baby boomers into something which is not only affordable but socially respectable.

> *I saw Anne Robinson the other day and she looks fantastic.*
>
> *I would have corrective eye treatment.*
>
> *If it was just for beauty I wouldn't but if it was for some medical reason then that is different. If it was just vanity then no.*
>
> *A lot of people would though. My wife would.*
>
> *I would not do plastic surgery, but face creams and all that sort of stuff . . . completely natural.*
>
> *I think you get to the stage, most people will try something as long as it did not involve cutting them or surgery.*

Evidence of a similar shift comes from America. A survey conducted in 2001 for the AARP found that half of American baby boomers are depressed that they're ageing. Eighteen per cent admitted to actively resisting it; 35 per cent of boomer women admitted to trying anti-ageing cosmetics; 53 per cent of boomer women and 6 per cent of boomer men admitted to using hair colour to hide their grey locks. One in ten American baby boomers, according to the AARP survey, is contemplating the radical step of cosmetic surgery.[22]

The idea that cosmetic plastic surgery has reached a 'tipping point' in the imagination of the British public is also backed by recent quantitative research. According to a survey published in January 2004, two-thirds of Britons want to change their looks with cosmetic surgery and one in ten have already gone under the knife. A full three-quarters of respondents to the survey believed that cosmetic surgery is more socially acceptable than it was five years ago.[23] Other figures suggest that the number of people in the UK trying to improve their image has increased six-fold in the past six years, with an estimated 25,000 surgical procedures performed. Much of that growth can be attributed to British baby boomers.[24]

Having their time again

If they'd had their time again, runs the wistful mantra of countless generations of older people, they'd be sure to make the most of it. What distinguishes the baby boomers is that they are determined to really have their time again – and are prepared to pay for the privilege. Younger baby boomers, it seems, are using their powerful consumer clout to buy up the best toys, and do popular culture in style. The average age of the owner of a Harley Davidson motorbike, for example, has accelerated from 38 to 46 in the last decade. The best-kept secret of the Harley brand is that its customers are more likely to be accountants and lawyers than unkempt hippies or ferocious Hell's Angels.[25]

Faith Popcorn recently identified the process whereby middle-aged baby boomers return to pursuits and products familiar from their youth as 'down-ageing'. The continued influence of younger baby boomers (those in their 40s) on popular culture has broader implications for the direction taken by young culture and popular culture. In his new book *Rock Till You Drop*, the American music journalist John Strausbaugh is scathing in his dismissal of the burgeoning market for 'colostomy rock' among American baby boomers. Rock music, he fulminates, 'simply should not be played by 55-year-old men, pretending still to be excited about playing songs they wrote 30 or 35 years ago and have played some thousands of times since. Its prime audience should not be middle-aged, balding, jelly-bellied dads who've brought along their wives and kids.'[26]

Evidence that baby boomers are determined to have their time again continues to abound in the UK. Model train maker Hornby recently reported a surge in profits as mature collectors snapped up its model railways and Scalextric racing car models last year.

Announcing that Hornby now sells 75 per cent of its trains to adults, Hornby chief executive Frank Martin said: 'There is a genuine resurgence in interest in our hobby ranges among adult collectors and enthusiasts. The demographic pattern of the postwar baby boomers entering their 40s and 50s with more time and disposable income than ever before gives real confidence that the current favourable market conditions will be sustainable for the foreseeable future.'[27]

But the idea that baby boomers are determined to have their time again goes far beyond a recherché interest in model railways. It is also about travelling, studying and doing all the things that they might have been too preoccupied or too lazy to do the first time around. Most baby boomers, it is worth pointing out, could not afford to own a Harley Davidson in their youth. Some, if they can remember much about their time at university, will have spent it in a haze of dope, fast-living and radical politicking. Others, preoccupied with the sudden arrival of a young family, were forced to ditch their dream to take an exciting adventure holiday. For many, the secret to having their time again is to do things properly, in style and at their own leisure.

For baby boomer grandparents, having their time again might even be about making up for the mistakes that they made with their own children. Researchers, for example, have discovered that British baby boomers are splurging a great deal of time and money on spoiling their grandchildren in a bid to play an active role in their upbringing. On average, the vast majority of Britain's 16.5 million grandparents expect to spend £64 each year on birthday and Christmas gifts, with 40 per cent willing to fork out on the deposit of a house or flat if asked. Of the 501 grandparents surveyed by the study, 85 per cent were happy to help out with loans while one-third already contribute financially towards the cost of clothes.[28] Not only does spending time with their grandchildren help baby boomers stay young and relive their own childhood. It seems it is also an opportunity to have their time again: to have a second crack at parenthood, this time without the distraction of having to spend long hours at the office to build a career.

The lure of nostalgia

Besides their attempts to stave off signs of physical decline and their obsession with the accessories of youth, baby boomers seem to be increasingly exorcising their fetish for youth culture in a more traditional way: nostalgia. A generation which once hoped to die before it got old, has, it seems, settled for postponing the inevitable by regressing to its youth.

The recent slew of nostalgia programming on both sides of the Atlantic is only the most obvious manifestation of how those in the media are targeting the memories of the middle-aged. Targeting the baby boomer generation is often most easily achieved by using music or celebrities which they remember from their youth. In America, the trickle of advertisers and marketers trying to communicate with boomers by jogging their memory has become a flood: Mercedes is using Janis Joplin songs; Cadillac has borrowed Led Zeppelin's 'Rock and Roll'; Pepsi has even persuaded Britney Spears to dress up in the kind of retro garb remembered by children of the 1960s.

An alternative route to capturing boomer nostalgia is for manufacturers to design souped-up versions of cult objects from boomer youth. DaimlerChrysler, for example, has recently revamped the old Thunderbird car as the PT Cruiser. And after its revamped Beetle, Volkswagen has decided to further capitalise on boomer nostalgia by resurrecting the Microbus Campervan. The company, which plans to make 80,000 of the vehicles per year, is betting on the fact that retired hippies who are now wealthy parents will pay to relive their youth. The van will retain its characteristic snub nose and pastel colours. But whereas the original Campervan was noisy and underpowered, the new model will have twenty-first-century upgrades including DVD players and four-wheel-drive.

Some advertisements, our interviewees acknowledged, connected more profoundly with them by using images from the past. More generally, there was a strong sense of our interviewees wanting to be 'in the know' – they delighted, for example, in recognising celebrities or music that younger people, or their children, don't recognise.

An ad I saw using Engelbert Humperdinck. I loved it, but my children didn't even understand why it was funny.

The second one was the Heineken advert on television; there is a Three Degrees song playing in the background which caught my ear. So it is basically humour, something connected, yes nostalgia with the Three Degrees. It almost sounds like I am pretty set in my ways.

I keep thinking of the Pepsi one . . . it is just because I can remember them on television when I was younger, a bit of nostalgia again.

Courting the boomer pound . . .

Beyond their complex relationship with the idea of youth, it is obvious that particular market sectors and approaches are set to profit at the hands of the ageing boomers. The travel industry, for example, is already profiting at the expense of the boomer wallet. According to the Travel Industry Association of America, for example, boomers travelled more often than any other age group in 2002, taking more than 241 million trips, or 44 per cent of the total. But the kind of holiday which boomers will expect may well be very different from that enjoyed by their parents. As consumers find themselves bombarded with the detritus of a lifetime's accumulation of goods, an influential new business idea suggests, they are increasingly losing interest in material possessions and reorienting themselves towards the purchase of experiences.[29] In her latest book, American marketing specialist Pamela Danziger argues that the real demographic force behind the shift from acquiring material things to the acquisition of experiences are baby boomers. The trend, she says, is evidenced in everything from the growth of 'adventure travel' and 'history travel' to a boom in 'adult-education experiences'.[30] So excited is the travel industry at the prospect of the baby boomers that it has invented a new marketing segment: the so-called 'bloomers' are late-flowering baby boomers who have the time and the inclination and the funds to travel.[31]

The cruise ship market, for example, has long been associated with the well-heeled but infirm, but, under the influence of the baby boomer generation, 'seniors cruises' are rapidly giving way to more dynamic, 'active holiday' alternatives aimed at the baby boomers. The re-jigging of the cruise concept for baby boomer customers gives a flavour of how the concerns and lifestyle pursuits of baby boomers differ from those of older generations. In the larger American market, cruise ships kitted out for baby boomers now regularly feature huge fitness centres with rock climbing walls, in-line skating, and even full-sized skating rinks within the ship itself. They come equipped with spas, massage therapists and other rejuvenation services. Particularly successful are lecture series which focus on educating passengers about an upcoming port of call.[32] In this country, it is worth noting that in the last decade the average age of the holidaymaker on a British cruise ship has fallen from 56.5 to 54.5.[33]

A surprising number of our baby boomer interviewees expressed the desire to move abroad in their old age, either to live out an active retirement or to take long holidays. Services which help boomers manage the process of moving abroad, for example, are likely to be warmly welcomed. Yet another area of growth is in education. Rather than a linear approach to life's goals, as we have seen, baby boomers appear to prefer a cyclical approach, dipping in an out of periods of education and work. Education and learning opportunities for boomers will have to be tailored to their needs, interests and hectic schedules.

> *You're not too old to do anything, I mean I was actually the youngest in the computer class . . . you know, that says something. People are . . . not trying to stay younger, but keeping themselves up to date, up with the modern things.*

When speculating on how baby boomers are likely to use their considerable purchasing power, however, much depends on how far those market sectors are prepared to innovate to meet boomer demands. Italy, for example, is the world's second most rapidly ageing society after Japan. Perhaps because of the strength of their numbers, older Italian consumers tend to be more confident about getting what they want. For the last five years, fashion designers Prada, Gucci and Armani have been offering special lines aimed at the older customer: complete with looser fits, higher waist and necklines and colours which accent pallid skin.[34] Car manufacturers in Japan and the US are finally waking up to the needs of the older consumer. In America, for example, Ford has unveiled futuristic features such as gauges with re-configurable fonts or type sizes designed for drivers with failing eyesight. The fact is that, at about age 45, most of us begin to experience age-related vision changes – including difficulty in focusing on near tasks such as reading, trouble distinguishing colours and contrast, and the need for more light. This is throwing up opportunities for creative designers in a wide range of industries. Lighthouse International, for example, a North American research and advocacy group for those with impaired vision, believes that advertisers are losing millions because ad designs contain print too small or too difficult to read. To highlight this, the organisation is publishing a series of free brochures to help educate businesses and organisations.[35]

Catering to the needs of an older constituency can pay rich dividends. Many Canadian publishers, for example, have enlarged their typeface in deference to baby boomers, and have profited as a result. Concessions to visually impaired older consumers, according to analysts, explains a 25 per cent increase in sales recorded in 1997 by map publisher Perly's for its large-type street directories of Montreal and Toronto.[36]

Case study – B&Q

The ageing population will present a challenge to many retailers in terms of how they can respond to a changing customer base and target market. Among others, DIY and gardening tool retailers will have to adapt to a combination of two trends – the ageing of the

UK population and the fact that older people tend to do more gardening than any other age group.

In the last decade, for example, a number of different considerations have catapulted B&Q to the role of standard-bearer in accommodating the needs of older people. In the first place, B&Q does not have a staff retirement age and is well known for employing older people – including, at the moment, one employee in his early 90s and several in their 80s. Being a retailer, the company is able to offer flexible and part-time work opportunities which are attractive to retirees. In the last few years, the number of employees over 50 at B&Q has increased from 15 per cent to 21 per cent of the workforce and those numbers are likely to continue to grow. One of the reasons for the success of this initiative is the fact that older employees tend to have previous DIY experience themselves and as a result are able to provide useful advice to customers.

Since around 1996, all new B&Q stores have been built with disability access and old stores were fitted with the same equipment. The company also began, in the late 1990s, to stock specialist products for older and disabled people. It soon discovered, however, that older people and disabled people don't like products made especially for them. As a result, and since 2001, it has been working with the Helen Hamlyn Research Centre at the Royal College of Art to develop inclusively designed DIY and gardening tools and now stocks a range of inclusively designed products. Those products include the 'Gofer', an electric screwdriver which is cordless, has a short head which is easy to grip and the 'Sandbug', an electric sander which is very light in weight, with a strap over the top and is thus easier to grip. In June 2004, the company published a booklet, *Inclusive Design Guidelines – towards usable products for everyone*, with the aim of outlining the principles which should inform designing for older people for its buyers and suppliers.[37]

... and how they want to spend it

Many baby boomers are currently at the peak of their earning careers. Many have recently benefited from, or are about to benefit from, windfall inheritances from their thrifty parents. A combination of factors makes them the wealthiest demographic group in contemporary society. Why then, are middle-aged people routinely ignored by marketers, advertisers and brand managers in favour of impressionable youth? A survey of 45,000 over-50s published in April by specialist marketing agency Millennium, for example, discovered that 86 per cent felt ignored by the marketing industry, and 70 per cent felt patronised by advertising.[38]

For most of the last decade, a debate has been raging within the advertising and marketing industry on whether it should adapt its efforts to accommodate the spending patterns of the so-called 'grey market'. Advocates of change argue that the baby boomers, unlike their parents when they were the same age, are fickle creatures whose spending patterns are no longer fixed at a young age. Sceptics, on the other hand, argue that the brand preferences of older people were shaped long ago, and that those in marketing and communications agencies should continue to focus on impressionable youth.

The first thing to note about the debate about the 'grey market' is that many of the advocates on both sides, working for advertising and marketing industries specialising in either youth or older people, have obvious axes to grind. The second point to recognise is that the idea of a 'grey market' is itself an incoherent category, referring as it does to everyone from 40 to 100. Marketers would never dream of segmenting the youth market with such sloppiness.

The baby boomers, however, are at the youthful end of the 'grey market'. Among the younger baby boomers that we interviewed (those between 40 and 50), our research uncovered a large degree of awareness of brands which are normally considered the preserve of young people.

I am a bit of a sucker . . . I would trust a company like Smirnoff

> *Vodka rather than a strange own label vodka. I would expect Smirnoff to be a better quality than a corner shop brand and I would expect to get less of a hangover with Smirnoff.*
>
> *I like Gap, I don't mind paying that bit extra if I know that it will last the whole year. I will only buy shoes from Clarks or Russell and Bromley because I know that they will last.*
>
> *For myself I will only wear Adidas trainers, I will never wear any other trainers. We have Sony everything – TV, video, camcorder – as we trust that brand.*

There was, among our younger boomer interviewees, much less evidence that they were turned off by excessive marketing. Generally advertising was regarded with a greater degree of playfulness and reflexivity and as something that could be enjoyed in its own right. There was also less of a desire to portray themselves as sensible consumers who were not influenced by advertising; they were happy to use advertising to their advantage.

> *I know it's a con, but I'm happy to play the game.*
>
> *They were also more likely to talk about adverts as something they were interested in and could enjoy for their humour or visual appeal.*
>
> *Baby boomers exhibit a different level of collusion with the marketing artifice. While they are more thoughtful consumers, they are more critical about the claims of marketers and retailers: they will reflect more, even if they usually do make the purchase. Young people, on the other hand, are just content to play the game, and collude with the artifice: they enjoy it, they don't need to self-consciously examine the claims of marketers. The boomers are a little more reflective, self-conscious and slightly more results-based in their evaluation of the claims of marketers. They ultimately collude, but it is not unthinking collusion but a reflective collusion.*
>
> Interview with Tamar Kasriel, Associate Director, The Henley Centre

The majority of our older boomers, however, claimed that they were now immune to the temptation to switch brands.

> *Over the years I have tried different things and I know what suits me so I just stick to the ones that I know.*

> *Adverts to me just do not work, period.*

Our research suggests that the changes in attitudes and behaviour which are suggested to typify the baby boomer generation are considerably less widespread among today's 50–60-year-olds. While the generation of 50–60-year-olds may have been at the forefront of social change throughout their lives, it seems to have been a minority within that group who challenged the norms and established new patterns of thought and behaviour. In contrast, the rest of their age group was probably quite similar to their parents. Change and the desire to be different were much more evident among our younger baby boomers, those aged between 40 and 50. We suggest that this younger group of baby boomers more widely reflects the attitudes generally associated with the baby boomer generation.

The debate in the advertising or communications industry about whether the consumer preferences of middle-aged people are fixed or fluid, however, is very limited in its scope – and obscures as much as it clarifies. What matters more than their susceptibility to seduction by marketers and advertisers is the different way in which baby boomers spend their cash. An influential avenue taken by contemporary political economy suggests that what is more important than the revealed preferences of consumers are the values which underlie and circumscribe those choices. What we need to understand, say many political economists, are the different uses that we have for money and the different roles or social relations which different forms of money take in different social contexts. Money which we have allocated for use in our retirement or for our children, for example, will not be used for gambling or vacations, and this is because we have allocated this money for a wholly different kind of role.[39]

This simple insight suggests that we enquire further into the values which underlie the purchasing decisions of baby boomers. And increasingly, research indicates, the priority of baby boomers is to seek to spend their money on themselves – to seek instant gratification of their needs and desires, and to spare no expense buying the kind of services and experiences which they deem relevant to the stage of life through which they are passing. It makes no sense to argue that the demand for these kinds of services and experiences has been fixed or determined in their youth.

> *As you grow older and you see things differently through wiser eyes, you tend to put things in different priorities and to me work comes bottom because work is just a way to a means and my means is getting the money from the work and spending it on things like travel and nice holidays.*

> *A nice way to frame the boomer fetish for instant gratification is their approach to religion. Whereas monotheistic religion invests in an afterlife and looks forward to it, the boomers invest in consumer spiritualities because they would prefer an immediate spiritual payoff to an investment in a highly uncertain afterlife. This is a highly consumerist rationality. It involves heavy discounting of the future in favour of immediate gratification.*
>
> Richard Tomkins, columnist, *Financial Times*

Other evidence suggests that baby boomers are refusing to defer gratification in order to save for their children. A recent survey by Henley Management College in the UK, for example, finds that already seven out of ten people who will retire in the next five years expect to use some or all of their capital to ensure that they have a comfortable and enjoyable retirement. The soon-to-be-retirees, according to the report, plan to treat themselves to holidays, cars and hobbies as well as paying for 'the basics' rather than save up a nest egg for their children.[40] While many of our respondents were concerned to make sure that their children were financially secure, others, more likely to be men, felt that their children should support themselves; these baby boomers were more at ease with the idea of spending their 'nest egg' entirely on themselves rather than giving some or all of it to their children.

Not everything. They can fend for themselves.

I haven't worked hard for 40 years to just give it all to my daughter.

I've three children. They've got good jobs, and they might turn around and say you know, we can make it, we've done it without the help from you, and now what you've got is yours, and you shouldn't go and spend it on us.

I've worked really hard, and I had to fight, and fight, and fight. And hands up, bugger it, I'm not going to leave it to them, I'm going to enjoy it. Because I've worked for that.

In America, advertisers are already poking fun at the tendency of baby boomers to spend the kids' inheritance. A recent ad for Sony, for example, opens in Seattle, where a Sony gadget freak in his 50s is learning Russian and visiting his lawyer to liquidate his assets. Then it begins to look sinister as he says goodbye to his kids and travels to Russia. By the time he blasts off into outer space courtesy of a Russian rocket, it's both an amazing spectacle and a shock. We see him floating around in his spacesuit, using his Sony video camera to record the view of Earth. 'When your kids ask where the money went,' it tells us, 'show them the tape.'[41]

However, baby boomers' expectation of 'spending the kids' inheritance' on themselves might be balanced out by their desire to spend money on their children while they are still alive. According to a recent survey conducted by MORI for the Joseph Rowntree Foundation more than half of home-owning parents of 18–29-year-olds said they didn't think their children would become home-owners without parental support. They would be willing and able to offer financial support, with most saying it would not have to be paid back.

They expect to give up to £24,000 to help their children get on to the housing ladder. In fact one in five parents said they would even borrow money themselves to help.[42]

For a generation which prides itself on being consumer savvy, it was instructive that only a tiny minority of our interviewees appeared to have done any financial planning for managing the inter-generational transfer of wealth – by setting up savings plans for their children's university education, or by thinking through how their retirement income would cover their and their children's needs. Our research suggests that opportunities exist to address more directly and unambiguously the issue of inter-generational wealth transfer, to offer products that meet the desire of parents to ensure their children are secure while also letting them enjoy the fruits of their labours in retirement. Here, service providers might well take the lead. A recent Datamonitor report, 'Marketing financial services to the over 50s', finds that many financial service providers in the UK are not catering to the growing number of consumers over the age of 50.[43] Given the often ambiguous attitudes among baby boomers to the inter-generational transfer of wealth, there is surely a great deal of scope for imaginative financial service providers to think up imaginative products aimed at solving their dilemmas.

The elasticity of youth

British people in their 40s now buy more albums than teenagers, according to recent figures published by the British Phonographic Industry. While the share of the market bought by teenagers has plummeted from 22.1 per cent to 16.4 per cent in only two years, the numbers of 40–49-year-olds has gone the other way in the same short period, rising from 16.5 per cent to 19.1 per cent.

The elasticity of youthfulness, it seems, is not limited to those 'born-again' bikers who are buying up Harley Davidsons. Beyond the figures produced by the music industry, a mountain of anecdotal evidence suggests that an invisible putsch is taking place within popular culture. Interviewed by a class of London schoolchildren in November 2003, our 51-year-old Prime Minister admitted to 'borrowing' from his children's CD collection, and confessed to his secret passion for rock band 'The Darkness'.[44] Earlier in the same year, magazine publisher David Hepworth had identified the rise of '50-quid man', the man in his 40s whose regular lunch-break splurges on albums and DVDs is increasingly keeping the beleaguered music industry in the black.[45] In truth, however, '50-quid man' is often a woman – the number of women buying albums and DVDs has been on the rise during the same period.[46] Similar figures are seen in America, where music industry analysts are intrigued by a new kind of pop singer (eg the 24-year-old piano-playing Norah Jones) whose best-kept secret is that their records are bought not by people their own age but by people old enough to be their parents.[47] In our conversations with baby boomers, many were at pains to point out their continued engagement with young culture.

> *When my mother was 40 she was old because I think for her generation when you got to 40 it was between the tweed, the twinsets, the pearls . . . whereas I'll listen to and enjoy the same music that my 13-year-old has. I like 'The Darkness', I like the hard rock, I'll listen to anything.*

If the baby boomers that we interviewed appear to have retained their fascination for the world of brands and popular culture, that is because they feel themselves to be still part of the youth culture. Many are simply refusing to pass on the baton of youth culture to young people, believing that since they invented it it remains rightfully theirs. Youth culture and popular culture, our research suggests, has expanded its boundaries – and now increasingly extends to encompass people in their 40s. In return, the content of much popular culture is beginning to reflect the interests of baby boomers. In America, for example, some major US brands have recently turned their back on risqué or overtly sexual advertising campaigns for fear of offending their more modest middle-aged consumers.[48] Some commentators have even linked the weight of baby boomers on popular culture to the furore which surrounded the recent baring of Janet Jackson's breast at the 2004 Superbowl.[49]

It suits those within the music industry and many baby boomers to keep this convergence of tastes quiet. But the shared interest in youth culture of baby boomers and their teenage offspring might well leave both too close for mutual comfort. In the coming years, as the centre of generational gravity shifts further towards middle age and the baby boomers redouble their efforts to master youth culture, we can expect some jostling for position between the two generations. The opening rounds in that battle are already being fought. In San Francisco, for example, Virgin Megastore recently removed shelves full of pop music to create a 'mind, body and spirit' zone to attract boomer customers. It has also expanded its jazz section and devoted displays to rock bands such as Led Zeppelin.[50] Clothing giant Gap, having recently lost the faith of its older consumers in a vain attempt to attract the younger market, is now suitably contrite, and is running ads which include older celebrities like Willie Nelson and singer Marianne Faithful singing boomer-friendly songs from the 1960s. Revved up by its own success, meanwhile, Harley is now saddled with the thankless task of attracting a younger generation of bikers while staying loyal to its flush middle-aged constituency.

Customisation and flexibility

For a good many years now, futurologists have waxed lyrical about the idea of 'mass customisation': the idea that mass production can be re-jigged – usually with the assistance of the one of the new technologies – to furnish consumers with a more personal and individualised service. As the boomers move their way into the centre of economic and political life, some of those claims may become a reality. Having grown up in a consumerist society, baby boomers are used to the responsiveness and personalisation of the consumer economy. It looks likely that they will demand a whole range of new and flexible consumer goods and services, not only customised to the needs of the individual boomer but also to their collective needs as ageing users. A recent survey of British baby boomers, for example, finds that 60.5 per cent of baby boomers, compared with 49 per cent of the older generation, claim that one of the most important factors in shaping their trust in public services is 'whether it meets their needs'.[51]

Asked to imagine the kind of bank or building society that they might wish for in 20 years' time, for example, our respondents placed a premium on service and flexibility.

> *They should accommodate you in every way possible. As much as they can. To be flexible. Not to bang on the charges whenever they feel it is necessary.*

The baby boomers will be a significantly more culturally and ethnically diverse generation of older people than their parents.[52] 'The important thing,' one of our interviewees suggested, 'is to get beyond the demographic, to appreciate how different one baby boomer is from the other.'[53] In our research, African-Caribbean and Asian respondents were all acutely aware of the shift in generations between their parents, themselves and their children, and more aware than others in our sample. Minority ethnic respondents talked of being brought up in what they described as a traditional, and often strict, manner, either in their native countries in the Caribbean or in Pakistan, or by first-generation immigrant parents here in Britain. They characterised their upbringing as heavily shaped by their native culture, and placed a priority on religious faith and respect for family. In our research among baby boomers, those in the minority ethnic group were keener than those in the other groups to favour 'traditional values' and to believe themselves to be the chief bearers of those values.

> *[We value] discipline, respect for elders, the courage to admit that you were wrong.*

> *We are the best of the last.*

Some of the group attributed these 'family values' to having been raised in Jamaica.

There, you have all your extended family.

Those in the group, however, were keen to point out that they had adapted to the English way of life.

We have adopted a more British way of life. We are better off financially.

I have no family back at home, my home is here now.

This kind of response should increase the pressure still further on businesses, public service providers and voluntary sector organisations to tailor their services to the individual needs of users. In the US, the voluntary sector has already taken a lead in this area. For example, the AARP tailors its services to the growing Hispanic population in the United States, not only offering a Spanish version of its website, but also a separate Spanish magazine for over-50s called *Segunda Juventud* (*The Second Youth*).[54]

Demands for customisation will also be fed by baby boomers' fluency with the new technologies. In the US, for example, the National Council on the Aging (NCOA) provides an online benefit calculator, www.benefitscheckup.org, which enables older adults to find out whether they are claiming all the benefits to which they are entitled. Once again in the US, the AARP offers online health information and expert advice through a dedicated 'Health and Wellness' section on its website (www.aarp.org/). Both schemes use online technologies to provide a customisation that would be impossible to deliver through conventional media.

According to MORI research, 69 per cent of British baby boomers are interested in undertaking learning activities in the future, more than double the figure for the current generation of older people.[55] It seems inevitable that there will be an increased demand among British baby boomers for flexible education, a flexibility which is only beginning to be addressed by organisations like the University of the Third Age in the UK.

Case Study – Senior Wellness Project, US

Many older adults suffer chronic health conditions which demand long-term treatment and support from health services and professionals. Through the active involvement of patients in the management and treatment of their respective conditions, their health and well-being can be improved as well as the need for professional medical care reduced.

The Senior Wellness Project is an initiative offered by a non-profit organisation called Senior Services in the Seattle and King County areas of the US. Its ultimate goal is to increase the health and quality of life of older people with chronic health conditions by getting older adults actively involved in their own healthcare. Through providing accessible and low-cost health promotion programmes, the project aims to complement the work of health services and professionals, increase effectiveness, reduce cost and provide a safe and supportive environment for people suffering chronic conditions. It is already working with about 3,000 older people in Seattle and King County.

The project operates on a number of appointed 'wellness sites'. Each site offers a range of different programmes, including the 'lifetime fitness programme', the 'health enhancement programme' and the 'living a healthy life' workshop. The 'lifetime fitness programme' is an ongoing exercise programme for older people which offers low-cost regular fitness classes for a wide range of physical abilities. The classes are taught by a trained fitness instructor and the programme attracts a wider range of older adults from diverse backgrounds. According to Susan Snyder, evidence-based studies of the programme show 'not only an increase in physical functioning [of participants] but participants were also less depressed and had less pain and were more socially active'.

The 'health enhancement programme' is a six-month programme that aims to create a partnership between the patient, physician (GP) and the health enhancement team to support the health and well-being of participants by getting them actively involved in their own healthcare. The health enhancement team consists of a registered nurse, a social worker and trained volunteer health mentors. Again, evidence-based studies of the programme showed that 'there was a 72 per cent decrease in hospitalisation and people took less medication.'

The 'living a healthy life workshop' is a six-week educational workshop that is intended to give participants the knowledge and tools to get involved in their own healthcare and manage their health more effectively. They are facilitated by older adults who have chronic conditions themselves.[56]

Customisation and the support economy

In contrast to their parents, baby boomers are often seen to be a fiercely independent and individualistic cohort. As a result, it is commonly held that the cohort is more inclined to trust themselves (to 'look after number one') more than each other or institutions.

> *I don't want to be reliant on anybody.*

More generally, we encountered a paradox at the root of this lack of trust among boomers. At the same time that they display a great deal of mistrust towards institutions and a great belief in doing things themselves, they seem much happier than any previous generation to pay for household services that make their lives easier.

> *I would be happy to contract a local tradesman, happy to pay for the service.*

> *A lot of people would rather have their groceries delivered by Tesco's or whatever it is and, perhaps they have earned the money to afford the luxury for them. I would rather pay somebody to paint my house and stay at work than I would have the time off to do it myself, personal thing.*

> *I would rather pay. Something I like doing, I do it myself, if I did not like doing it, if I was financially able I would rather pay somebody to do that on my behalf.*

A recurrent theme of our research, when baby boomers were asked to collage their vision of their lives in the future, was the hope that things would become simpler and less 'cluttered' – both in a material and in an emotional sense. Many looked forward to a 'pared-down' home environment, where life was still very comfortable, but where there would be less people and less 'stuff', especially less of their children's possessions and clutter. For our boomer interviewees, too ample a palette of options can be confusing and increase the sense of anxiety about making the wrong choice or differentiating between too broad a panoply of choices. In other words, while the baby boomers were more enthusiastic than any older generation to be handed the reins of choice, they also recognised the limits of choice.

One emerging route around this paradox might lie in the emerging business idea of a 'support economy'. In their recent book *The Support Economy*, the American business scholars James Maxmin and Shoshana Zuboff argue that twenty-first-century capitalism will be governed by a new business logic in which federated groups of companies will pool their resources to offer genuinely personalised, 'deep' support to a new breed of busy consumer – they will get together to take the hard work out of choosing and will act as gatekeepers, helping consumers to navigate through the minefield of organising their lives.[57]

Much as the baby boomers are suspicious about the motives of large organisations, their enthusiasm for purchasing consumer solutions means that they seem destined to place their trust in a small number of corporate gatekeepers to look after their own interests. The idea of a 'support economy' may well throw up new opportunities for canny corporations, which may want to add a customised web of highly personalised support services to their customer service offering: offering to do everything from babysitting their grandchildren to walking their dog. Any service or communication which can give the impression that it has 'done the hard work for them', for example, by searching for the best deal or by picking out the most important features for comparison, is likely to be warmly welcomed. The phenomenal growth of home assistance services is, according to an emerging consensus, attributable to the demography of an ageing society. While past ad recoveries were fuelled by strong retail and automotive sectors, a report published by research firm Global Insight has concluded that the next wave of ad growth will shift to service-oriented businesses – entertainment, cosmetics and financial-services companies – as advertisers try to reach the ageing baby-boomer population.[58]

> *If someone's offering to sort it out for you . . . yes.*
>
> *Take the burden. Not the financial burden, but the burden of getting everything paid on time.*
>
> *Helping you with your homes [would be useful] because a lot of us live in old homes with no facilities.*

Case study – British Gas and 'here to HELP'

Many of today's older people in the UK live in poverty and lack access to essential services. Partnerships between public, voluntary and private sector service providers offer one way of addressing this issue. Launched in 2002, 'here to HELP' is a unique collaboration between British Gas, social housing providers and seven national charities, including Help the Aged, to improve housing conditions and quality of life for people in deprived areas across the UK. The 'here to HELP' programme is funded and managed by British Gas, with additional funding from the local partner social housing providers. The programme aims to reach around 500,000 households with its unique, holistic range of services.

Working locally, British Gas and the housing providers

collaborate to set up special 'HELP Zones' in areas of deprivation. Each 'HELP Zone' contains around 500 homes, and each home is visited by a specially trained team of surveyors who make a detailed survey of the condition of the property. Eligible households will then receive free energy efficiency work, including loft and cavity wall insulation, draught proofing, hot water tank jackets and lighting, to make their homes more efficient, warmer and cheaper to heat. This is supplemented by a free benefits health check, to ensure that clients are claiming all the money that is available to them.

In addition to this, the surveyors also conduct a 'quality of life' check, to assess whether the client can benefit from help from any or all of the seven charities which are each offering free products and services through the scheme. Help the Aged itself offers a wide range of free services (funded by British Gas) through the programme, including the SeniorLink community alarm service, the SeniorLink information line and their award-winning range of information booklets, covering over 30 topics from financial advice to medicine management. However, the primary service offered by Help the Aged is the HandyVan scheme, which installs security devices (door locks, window locks, smoke alarms, door chains and spy-holes) in the homes of older people to make them safer and more secure.

By the spring of 2004, Help the Aged had received over 14,000 referrals to its services, many from clients previously not reached by the charity. As well as its sheer scale, the main advantage of 'here to HELP' is the unique range of services that, working together, the partners can provide. Many clients have benefited from the services of more than one charity, and older people in particular can receive help from Help the Aged, Scope and the RNIB, as well as the energy savings and extra income from the benefits health check. According to Louise Parkes of Help the Aged, this is what makes the programme special: 'the unique strength of "here to HELP" is in its collaborative nature. By working in partnership, we are able to provide a more holistic range of solutions than any one organisation acting alone.'[59]

How to talk to the boomers

Nothing illustrates better the prickly sensibilities of some baby boomers than asking them what they want to be called. When an advertising agency recently enquired of American baby boomers how they wished to be addressed as a collective group, it rapidly came unstuck. 'Senior' was rejected by 98 per cent of respondents, while 85 per cent turned up their noses at the term 'older adult'. Nearly three-quarters like to see themselves as 'middle-aged' and two-thirds didn't even like the denomination 'baby boomers'. Even relatively mild euphemisms, such as 'active adult' and '50-plus', are rejected by a clear majority of the over-50 crowd.[60]

Within all this all this lies an important lesson for those charged with communicating with baby boomers. Paramount among the concerns of baby boomers, as we have seen, is a desire not to be patronised, dictated to or condescended to by those in authority. All of this presents challenges for those in the marketing and communications industry, who may be enlisted to nudge idealistic baby boomers into thinking about their 'old old' age so that they are prepared and able to deal with it in the best way possible. At the very least, it seems, the ageing of the baby boomers looks likely to give rise to issues of tone and etiquette for communications professionals. In the US, the boomer fetish for youthfulness means that marketers are increasingly disguising boomer products which are associated with ageing or infirmity: hearing aids, eyeglass lenses, etc. Makers of bifocal reading glasses, for example, are pandering to boomer narcissism by attempting to disguise the function of age-related products which might otherwise scare its boomer customers. Take an ad for bifocal contact lenses. Rather than associating bifocals with the deterioration of age, the 50-something woman in a recent ad for Acuvue contact lenses says, 'Think of it as upgrading your contacts.'

More recently in the US, a national initiative designed to educate baby boomers about hearing problems has hired the veteran rock star Pat Benatar to front an 'It's Hip to H.E.A.R.' campaign.[61]

> *You do not want to be spoken to as an 'old person'.*
>
> *Nobody has yet cracked the idea of how to sell to baby boomers. The problem is consistently one in which boomers don't like to see older people in ads, but at the same time they hate seeing 15-year-olds as well. My suggestion: to find different icons, to change the discourse surrounding youth and ageing. The holy grail is to suggest age without suggesting that people have aged.*
>
> Interview with Tamar Kasriel, Associate Director, The Henley Centre

Rather than being presented with a commercial narrative or image, older baby boomers also appear to like being presented with useful and objective facts. Indeed, consumers *claim* that they want straightforward communication that tells them the facts and allows them to make up their own minds about things. Across our groups, 'home-made' or 'amateur' leaflets for services such as local builders or garden shops were frequently cited as examples of preferred communications styles which subscribed to this ideal of 'straight talking'. In addition, straightforward communications that talked about price or saving money were frequently praised as they allowed people to 'know where they stand'. A good example of what might work, suggested by one respondent, was a brief guide to wines by the supermarket group J Sainsbury. Not knowing much about wine, our interviewee appreciated the simple and apparently impartial explanation and advice about wine's suitability for different occasions.

The individualist, non-conformist boomers also loved to laugh at communication. We encountered evidence that they appreciate a down-to-earth and possibly self-deprecating humour, and a readiness to laugh at and appreciate any deliberate attempt *not* to be cool. Indeed, laughing at the idea of ageing might be cathartic for this generation. It may be that their anxieties about ageing are best communicated through humour, through an approach that self-consciously seeks to subvert the traditional ideas and symbols of ageing.

> *The one that really tickles me at the moment is the Vauxhall advert where you have the two kids saying 'are you grown up?' and I just think that is absolutely funny.*
>
> *And the other one is when a girl comes into the room and mum and dad are fighting over some sweets and it's, 'it will all end in tears, give up,' and she's being the mother and the parents are being the children.*

In America, where advertising aimed at baby boomers is more common, Danone is only the latest advertiser to make fun of the idea that the new generation of middle-aged attention-seekers might end up embarrassing their strait-laced children. North American ads for the company's latest yoghurt LaCrème feature a racy midlife scenario with a woman in a maid outfit spoon-feeding yoghurt to a middle-aged guy while sitting on his lap. When a teenager suddenly walks into the hallway with her friend, she retreats, obviously embarrassed, before mumbling to her friend, 'My parents are so weird.'[62]

Given the cynicism of baby boomers towards established institutions, it was hardly surprising that our baby boomers preferred to have their purchasing guided by their friends and colleagues rather than rely on mass-market advertising. We asked our interviewees, 'How would you like to find out about new products when you're older?'.

> *I'd ask my mate.*
>
> *I'd ask my son.*
>
> *Word of mouth.*
>
> *Personal recommendation.*

4. Science, technology and well-being

What role do science and technology play within the lives of British people, and what role would they like them to play in their future? The majority of baby boomers have already used computers in the workplace, and will have no need of the basic training which today's elderly might require. But both inevitable physical decline and the lack of trust among baby boomers will play a role in determining the kind of technology that they will want to use.

Existing research suggests that the baby boomers are very happy to email, to search the internet and to use their mobile phones. Baby boomers are almost as keen as younger generations on new media technologies. Thus, according to research from MORI, 88.5 per cent of baby boomers and 94.5 per cent of 15–34-year-olds own mobile phones, compared with only 73 per cent of 55–64-year-olds and 49 per cent of the over-65s. Moreover, 69.5 per cent of baby boomers and 69 per cent of 15–34-year-olds use the internet, compared with only 51 per cent of 55–64-year-olds and 17 per cent of the 65+ age group.[63] As a large number of baby boomers find that 'computers and other modern electronic devices are good fun', MORI forecasts that their usage of modern technology is set to increase even further as they continue to age.[64]

> *We have seen a rise in the level of internet usage in the over-50 population as a whole from detailed research and visits to the*

Saga website. Those below retirement age and still working may be influenced by the use of new technologies in the workplace and realise the benefits to individuals at home. With retirement comes the time, money and growing confidence to explore old and new hobbies and the internet makes information accessible at the click of a button.

Emma Reid, Head of Customer Information,
Saga Group[65]

For most of our baby boomer interviewees, however, the new technologies present themselves as a double-edged sword. Most acknowledged that technology aims to make our lives easier, saving us time or energy at home and in the workplace. Some appreciated that increasing computerisation might even mollify some of the problems which they associated with old age:

Why sit there and lose your eyesight when you could just tell the computer when you want the curtains to close, and they'll close them. Get on the computer and say I want the Halifax, I want my money please and it'll come up on that website without you having to do anything.

I can see us having a home where you tell the computer when you want the kettle to boil, or you want the lights on . . . your house will be computerised, you just need to tell it what to do, and it'll be done. But it won't do the ironing!

I could ring the microwave to tell it to put the dinner on.

Technology accepters vs technology laggards

Broadly speaking, attitudes to technology among our baby boomer interviewees differed according to age. Our younger baby boomers were more prone to thinking creatively into the future about possible developments in technology and the advantages which they might bring – voice-activated home appliances, for example. They anticipated that the internet would continue to play an important role in their lives, allowing them to pursue their interests and keep in touch with others. Many were excited by the opportunities that the new technologies offered for increased convenience and communication. There was also a widespread feeling that using the internet, texting on their phone, etc, helped to keep them connected in a broader sense – in touch with their irrepressible youth, and in tune with what's going on in the world. They were knowledgeable about technology and tended to see it as an enhancement to their quality of life rather than an imposition. The exception to this was the group of Asian women and some men in lower-income groups – who were largely inexperienced with and uninterested in the internet but who were considerably more positive about mobile phones. One Asian woman we interviewed, for example, used email extensively on her television through Sky and considered this rather than the internet as the most accessible new technology.

Among our older baby boomer interviewees, on the other hand, several were considerably less at ease with new technologies. About half of them were rather positive about the use of the internet and email, or could at least see its value in offering greater ease, greater convenience as well as the chance to stay in touch with family and friends abroad. This half of the older group of boomers tended to deem the rise of new technologies inevitable and therefore believed that they should try to get used to it in order not be left behind. When it came to internet usage, such 'technology accepters' among older baby boomers tended to use the internet for researching and communicating with friends and family rather than for buying goods or services.

> *In terms of finding holidays, in terms of looking for new music, new books and in terms of keeping in touch with people.*

It was these people who tended to be happiest using mobile phones, although there was a feeling that mobiles were complicated and offered a range of functions which they found to be unnecessarily confusing, and which got in the way of using the phone for its central purpose – making calls. These people expressed interest in simpler mobile phones – a 'back to basics' approach that would simply allow them to make and receive calls and text. They anticipated that they would particularly appreciate this when they were older and finding mobiles too fiddly or baffling to use. Their responses suggested that the manufacturers of mobile devices might begin to make different devices for the different needs of different demographics.

The remaining half of the 50–60-year-olds were what we might call 'technology laggards'. They were very negative about computers, the internet and mobile phones. Many were simply resigned to being left behind.

> *Where do you buy an MP3? As far as I know, it is something that you download and you make a compilation of things.*

The defensiveness of some of our older baby boomers probably arises out of frustration that they don't understand new technologies or are unable to use them properly. It is a frustration which seems to reinforce their perception that the world is beginning to pass them by. Many among them described mobile phones as complicated, confusing or unnecessary and although many had them and were using them they appeared to do so begrudgingly. Their preferred reaction to what they took to be the accelerating pace of technology was to opt out of the race.

> *By the time all this has happened, we'll be gone.*

Both younger and older baby boomers, however, were keen to admit that in this area there was still a generation gap – that they lagged behind their children in understanding how the internet works. Furthermore, many admitted that their children had become their technology gurus:

> *I pick up most of the new stuff from my kids. It kind of leaks into our lives.*

My children blind me on the internet.

Computerisation and the personal touch

While many of our baby boomer interviewees were enthusiastic about the new technologies, their accumulated experience of those technologies had led many to the conclusion that technology can increase stress – either because it encourages the 'speeding up' of time or because our reliance upon it leaves us helpless. Most importantly, many were concerned that increased computerisation and automation often serve to make life more impersonal. Our subjects were resigned to a future dominated by new technology, but were not convinced that increased computerisation and mechanisation would make life easier.

Talking to banks now is talking to a machine.

I see a vision of having ten different remote controls. It's not service; it's not personal.

All of our baby boomer respondents felt it imperative that computerisation was not used to minimise personal contact and personal service. This was particularly important for older baby boomers – who were horrified at what they saw as increasingly depersonalised approaches to customer service. The use of digital phone menus, they felt, was the ultimate expression of this and something which they found time-consuming, frustrating and confusing:

I tried to get hold of someone today on the phone, but the service said 'If you know the number, press 1'.

How many times do you sit there trying to work out your credit card bill, you ring up about your gas bill and have to press 1 then 2, then they cut you off and you have got to start all over again.

I still want to retain the personal touch.

We want to speak to the operator.

We want to go directly to the source.

Some were adamant that the service suppliers ought to be properly trained:

You should be treated with courtesy by professionals who are trained in that field.

For some, it was important to speak to people who were not too young:

At least we wouldn't have 18-year-olds telling us what to do all the time.

Baby boomers, it seems, are alive to the possibilities thrown up by new technology, but are equally alert to the fact that many companies are using those new technologies solely to cut costs. These are service demands which some companies are already responding to. Some are already reaping the rewards of doing so. But much more can be done, both by public and private sector bodies, to get the blend of human and machine right within service provision.

The security hurdle

There is already good evidence that British baby boomers will not embark on using advanced technology without being convinced of its usefulness and security. Existing studies, for example, suggest that the prevalence of internet shopping is far lower among boomers than among younger people.[66] Our research provided further evidence that when risks are involved and the advantages unclear, boomers remain wary about internet security.

I hate giving out my credit card number on the internet.

If I book a holiday, I prefer a travel agent.

I would not buy anything over the internet.

You read about all types of flaws with internet banking so it would make me nervous.

They all say it's secure but I am a bit dubious.

Since many of those baby boomers who have embraced the new technology are not yet using it for financial transactions, there is an obvious need to find a new language, a need to provide reassurance on security. Even many boomer technophiles were reluctant to use the internet to make their purchases because of existing worries about security of their personal data.

A tool, not a toy

Beyond any practical differences in how baby boomers make use of new technologies, our research suggested that technology appears to play a different role within the lives of baby boomers than it does within youth culture. It was simply a highly functional means to an end – communicating with absent loved ones or a research tool – and not something which warranted being experimented with or played with for its own sake.

I think keeping in touch is one thing, I mean [all talking] I can send an email but I can't sit on it for four or five hours every night, I'd rather read a book.

The vast majority prioritised the idea of keeping in touch. The importance of hobby-based websites and chat-rooms is likely to increase as the boomers age and more time becomes available to them. Crucially, however, many of our respondents were concerned that the new technologies would only add to their sense of exclusion from the wider community.

Shopping on the web instead of going out and meeting people means you could get very lonely.

A few were cynical enough to suggest that increased automation and computerisation might be used by government only to make savings in the services that it was obliged to provide them.

> *They are trying to shy away from personal contact. It is easier for them.*

Accessibility and the idea of universal design

> *Baby boomers would rather be able to use a mainstream product, which accommodates them and doesn't look like some kind of geriatric device.*
>
> Michelle Sohn, Senior Product Manager, OXO International

As the boomers grow into old age, physical impairments will eventually become an obstacle to computer usage. In 2003, for example, Microsoft US commissioned Forrester Research to investigate the impact of the 'wide range of abilities and its impact on computer technology' in 2003. Of working-age people, it found that roughly one in four (27 per cent) have a visual difficulty or impairment; that one in four (26 per cent) have a dexterity difficulty or impairment; that one in five (21 per cent) have a hearing difficulty or impairment; that one in five (20 per cent) have cognitive difficulty.

All the evidence suggests that baby boomers will want to use non-patronising, highly accessible technology which mitigates the inevitable effects of ageing: diminishing eyesight, hearing and physical dexterity. Any such technology providers, however, will be forced to account for the unwillingness of boomers to be pigeonholed as 'old'. One emerging solution to the problem is to conceal technological solutions to boomer infirmity in a universal design aesthetic which, at least in theory, can be appreciated across the generations. Following its research programme into obstacles to computer usage, for example, Microsoft US built into its Windows XP operating system accessibility options such as using large icons and transforming text into speech when users have real problems seeing the screen. It has also incorporated an 'Accessibility Wizard' into Windows XP, allowing the user to customise Microsoft programs according to their individual needs. For example, the cursor size and blink-rate can be adjusted, font sizes and colours can be altered beyond previous specifications, and visual and sound notification can be added to many functions. Although relatively minor, these modifications can make a positive difference to everyday use – especially for those with failing eyesight.[67] They are published on Microsoft's US website with the title 'Tips for baby boomers on the awkward age of computing'. They feature cartoons and treat the reality of ageing as an easily surmountable hurdle which does not have to change one's way of life.

Microsoft is not the only computer manufacturer to see the business case for working towards the design needs of an ageing society. Many of the above features have been available on Apple's operating systems for a number of years.[68] Working along similar lines, Hewlett Packard now produces keyboards with illuminated keys and printers with backlit LCD displays to improve vision accessibility. And together with many other computer manufacturers, Hewlett Packard also make wireless hardware connected by infrared ports, all of which helps to increase general mobility.[69] Other widely available computer innovations include large-key multicoloured keyboards, screen magnifiers, touch-sensitive computer screens and text readers which translate text into speech.[70]

The chief bugbear of our baby boomer interviewees, however, was not the desktop computer but the mobile phone, which seemed to them to become more petite and more complicated every year. Here, it seems, much remains to be done by the mobile industry. An example of good industry practice, however, comes from Japan, where the marketers at Japanese telecoms company NTT DoCoMo have launched a new mobile phone specifically aimed at the older consumer. Called 'Raku-Raku', or 'easy-easy', it has a panel with larger buttons and easier-to-read figures. The phone, which features larger easier-to-read letters for email and a simplified automatic dialling system, has been a huge hit among Japanese baby boomers: over

200,000 units were sold in less than two months. The most important lesson to be learned when selling new technology to boomers, the marketing manager of NTT DoCoMo who developed the 'Raku-Raku' told *Associated Press*, is never to let on that the product is targeting them. 'If you push it as a grandpa and granny phone, it won't work,' he said. 'Its concept is a cell phone for beginners.'[71]

But a universal design aesthetic need not concern itself exclusively with new technology. Many of the most significant innovations in the field have been relatively simple: voice-activated electronic organisers, for example, or easy-to-use calculators.[72] There are steps which local authorities can take to make public space more accessible and easier to navigate – some of which are already commonplace. Steep steps, for example, can be replaced by or supplemented with gentler slopes, which can be fitted with panels to improve traction.[73]

Case study – OXO International, United States

Most household and gardening tools are designed for the average young adult who has no dexterity problems or disabilities. However, this excludes all those from the mainstream market who do not conform to the average. The concept of inclusive design emerged in order to provide for this large segment of users. According to RICS (Research Institute for Consumers Affairs), the goal of inclusive design is 'to design mainstream products and services so as many people as possible can use them'.[74] Tools designed according to inclusive design principles aim to be easily useable for the widest range of people by taking into account in the design process as many potential needs and dexterity problems that a user might have.

All OXO products are based on the principles of inclusive design. For OXO this means 'designing products for young and old, male and female, left- and right-handed and many with special needs'. However, for OXO to adhere to the standards of universal design not only means designing products for as many users as possible, but also making sure that OXO products are affordable for the broadest range of customers possible. As Michelle Sohn puts it: 'For us universal design includes the price. So, we don't want to be the most expensive product on the market. We haven't raised our retail prices in 12 years. So, having an accessible price is part of it too. The product should be easy to use, accessible and comfortable, but it should also be attainable.'

OXO was founded by a retired American, Sam Farber, in the late 1980s, when he discovered that his arthritic wife was having trouble with a number of kitchen tools. Spurred out of retirement by the incident, Farber, together with an US industrial design company called Smart Design, began to create kitchen tools that would be comfortable and easy to use for people of all ages and abilities. As part of the design process they worked together with chefs, home cooks, ergonomics experts, gerontologists and the elderly themselves and in 1990 the first range of 'OXO Good Grips kitchen tools' appeared on the US market.

However, when Sam Farber and Smart Design developed the first product range, they realised that to be successful they would have to appeal to all generations. According to OXO's senior product manager Michelle Sohn, they had to 'make them look fresh and young and hip and cool, so our whole target market wouldn't only be people with dexterity problems or older people'.

Several considerations figured in this decision. One of them was that if OXO products were intended only for people with dexterity problems or older people, they would not reach a large enough target market. Moreover, OXO recognised that many older adults don't want to be categorised and tagged as such. They would, says Sohn, 'rather be able to use a mainstream product, which accommodates them and doesn't look like some kind of geriatric device'. Although the products are specifically labelled as 'easy-to-use', the company refuses to market its products specifically at older adults and people with dexterity problems. However, as part of its research and development programme OXO integrates potential users into the design process from a very early stage.[75]

5. Information, advice and trust

Baby boomers tend to be characterised as an 'untrusting' cohort, wary of everything from institutions to authority to the motives behind marketing pitches. To some extent, this is part of a more general 'deficit of trust' which cuts across the demographic spectrum, and we must be careful not to attribute it solely to the boomers.[76] Nevertheless, there is good evidence that boomers are particularly reluctant to put their trust in other people and in public institutions.

A MORI poll on trust in public institutions published in 2003, for example, painted a stark picture of British boomers and their approach to public services. The boomers, the data suggested, are not impressed by rhetoric alone but concentrate on outcomes and performance. When asked the question 'What are the most important factors in determining how much trust you have in public services?' for example, 60.5 per cent of baby boomers compared with 49 per cent of the older generation and 56 per cent of the younger generation answered, 'Whether services meet your needs'. Fifty-six per cent of baby boomers compared with 49 per cent of older and 53 per cent of younger answered, 'How you are treated by staff'.[77]

The poll asked respondents whether they agreed or disagreed with statements that 'senior public service managers are . . .':

- Honest – 35.5 per cent of baby boomers disagree

compared with 28 per cent of older people and 27.5 per cent of younger people

- Trustworthy – 36.5 per cent of baby boomers disagree compared with 26.5 per cent of older generations and 29.5 per cent of younger generations
- Competent – 20.5 per cent of baby boomers agree compared with 28 per cent of older generations and 27 per cent of younger generations.

What these responses suggest is that British baby boomers have higher expectations of service provision than both younger and older generations, and that they are more reluctant to put their trust in public service managers. More generally, most of our boomer interviewees were extremely loath to put their trust in government or other institutions:

> *The media lies.*

The uphill struggle which government faces in winning the trust of baby boomers was amply demonstrated when our baby boomer interviewees were asked to evaluate schemes which might improve their quality of life. Many saw the schemes as a simple example of cost-cutting by automation and routinisation.

> *That is easy for government. They are just trying to get out of their responsibilities. Next thing, you will see a little box delivered, saying 'Monday's dinner', 'Tuesday's dinner'.*

Asked about an innovation which might allow them to live in a 'barrier-free' city, the subjects were distinctly underwhelmed and more than a little suspicious.

> *It looks like Milton Keynes.*
>
> *It's about control. They simply want to dump us.*

Trust and consumerism

The general lack of trust among baby boomers also has implications for their consumer behaviour. Asked to think of examples of brands or companies that they trust or rely on, our baby boomer interviewees mentioned a number of long-standing household names, including Marks and Spencer, Heinz, Tesco, Asda, John Lewis, the AA, Clarks Shoes, Virgin, Colgate and the BBC (although some of these were also given by others as examples which they didn't trust). These brands obviously offer a sense of familiarity, appealing to baby boomers' sense of nostalgia.

> *BT, because they have been there for years; they do seem to offer a good service.*
>
> *Palmolive soap, I've really trusted in that for years and years.*
>
> *I don't believe that just because you pay more you are going to get a better product or a better service but there are some things like Oil of Ulay you cannot beat. My mum used that as well when she came here and she looks very well for her age.*
>
> *Heinz: it has been around for so long.*

Commonly, respondents viewed that trust can only come from experiencing the brand.

> *I think you can only trust after you build up a rapport. I do not think you can trust something or somebody or a product until you've actually tried.*
>
> *Sainsbury's is a very trustworthy supermarket and it works and is the same all the time. I have experienced consistency throughout and that is what I would call trust.*

The words most often associated with trusted commercial brands were 'consistency', 'quality', 'safety', 'reliability', 'value for money' and 'being around for a long time', 'nothing is too much trouble' and the idea that 'it hasn't let me down'.

> *The freshness, the taste of them, it doesn't change and alter.*

> *Heinz . . . It's just because it never ever changes.*

Trust, once again, seems to have a great deal to do with high levels of service.

> *I was thinking about the watch, the Rolex, I mean you can trust it. It's quality. If anything goes wrong, they put it right.*

Other reasons for picking brands or organisations they trust included expertise or efficiency and accuracy in dealing with requests, problems, customer service queries, etc, going beyond the call of duty or a sense of being looked after; a sense of value for money or of not being ripped off; a service that treats you as an individual, listens and responds to your needs. A reason given for not trusting in a brand or organisation was a lack of expertise or attention to you as an individual patient or consumer.

Trust in science and new technologies

Among our baby boomer interviewees, there was ample evidence of a lack of trust in, or suspicion about, science and technology. Baby boomers, for example, revealed ongoing concerns about everything from the security of financial transactions on the internet to questions over the safety of GM foods. If this prickly demographic is to be at ease with technology and to embrace its benefits, it will be necessary to confront those fears. It is worth noting that the same baby boomers who were generally suspicious of the idea that the progress of science and technology makes the world a better place were happy to consider using it to keep themselves alive or to chase the elixir of their lost youth.

> *Medical technology can really help the world. I don't think having a bigger, smaller, flatter screen is really going to make*

that much difference to me in 20 years' time; however, I do think technology can help with the medical world.

That paradox, we assume, might be of use to those in the science and technology fields as they go about selling their wares to sceptical baby boomers. For example, the same baby boomers who are hostile to genetic modifications of food in order to improve agricultural productivity might become highly enthusiastic about gene-based treatments which purport to slow the ageing process. At the end of May, for example, it was reported that scientists from cosmetics giant L'Oreal had identified the genes which play a role in turning our hair grey, and were working on possible treatments.[78] Faced with such temptations, baby boomers may be unable to resist.

Information-seekers

British baby boomers, as we have seen, are highly reluctant to trust either institutions or authority figures to provide them with information and advice. Increasingly, however, they are happy to place their trust instead in the library of searchable information on the World Wide Web. Research commissioned by Pfizer Australia, for example, showed that boomers researched conditions and treatments on the internet and were willing to challenge their doctors with the information they discovered.

As we have already seen, our research evidenced a perception (especially felt among some of our lower-income interviewees and Asian women interviewees) that GPs were either out of touch with the concerns of their patients or lacking in empathy. As a result, some of our interviewees claimed to prefer to use internet-based research or word-of-mouth health advice as a means of addressing health problems, especially those relating to their children.

You can get a lot of good information from the internet, on HRT for example. You don't use it blindly: you can get different opinions.

But how, we asked, would they evaluate those opinions?

> *It's a gut instinct.*

The tendency among individualistic boomers to mistrust medical professionals and 'self-treat' aches and pains – often using unverifiable information gleaned from the internet – has its own dangers. Some medical sociologists have voiced concerns that boomers who 'self-treat' medical conditions could end up causing themselves real harm.

6. Care, dependence and support services

Far from the media stereotype, older baby boomers are often identified by demographers as a 'pivot generation' or a 'sandwich generation' – one which is often struggling to juggle the demands of their jobs with looking after elderly parents and children or grandchildren. A recent report funded by the Joseph Rowntree Foundation, which surveyed more than 1,000 over-50s, found that two-thirds are in paid employment while six out of ten 50-year-olds have living parents and a third have grandchildren. As many as one in three looked after an elderly relative or friend, one in six provided care for a grandchild and one in ten did both. Few of the employees interviewed wanted to give up their jobs in order to take on caring responsibilities but some grandparents were prepared to give up work or reduce their hours to look after their grandchildren. Many said their caring roles gave them a sense of satisfaction but almost half said it had made their life more stressful.[79]

Care and the changing shape of the family

The fact that many baby boomers are now caring for elderly parents is a constant reminder of the kind of care which they might need in their old age. Will baby boomers expect to receive the same care in their old age which they are currently providing to their parents? The importance of the family as caregiver should not be underestimated. Back in 1993, a study by the Institute of Actuaries estimated that the value of care given to older people by family and friends amounts to £33.9 billion annually.[80] Currently, two-thirds of care provided for older people continues to come from within the family.[81]

The role of the caregiver is only likely to become more indispensable as boomers' independence and distrust of institutions combine to make family and home care more desirable – even if it will decrease in duration as boomers stay healthy for longer. Danish longitudinal research suggests that family care will sit well with baby boomers. They do, according to the Danish research, see family as being more important than their counterparts did 10–15 years ago and wish to spend more time with their families. This boomer affinity for family life remains true in other areas. George Leeson of the Oxford Institute of Ageing, for example, points to the increase in inter-generational travel as an illustration of how boomers would rather spend money travelling with their children now instead of saving it for their inheritance.[82]

There are some important paradoxes here. In the first place, increased longevity and decreasing fertility mean that the family is extending vertically at the same time as it is being compressed horizontally. The rise of the so-called 'beanpole family' will mean an increase in the number of living generations and a decrease in the number of living relatives within these generations. Since we are less and less likely to have lots of family members of our own age, the bulk of the care burden will weigh on the shoulders of single family members. Research shows that this is a role still played primarily by women[83] – it is they who are most willing to give care and it is from them that older people would most like to receive it. But as women gain an increasing foothold in the modern workplace, this may not be feasible and workable as a long-term arrangement.

Other social and demographic changes may conspire to threaten the aspiration of boomers to be cared for in their own home. While the immediate family may become compressed horizontally, extended families of different shapes are becoming the norm. People often have more than one marriage and children by different partners. A recent Open University report states that the incidence of divorce in the UK is now the highest in Europe – approximately one-third of marriages end in divorce after 20 years.[84] The implication seems to be that intergenerational family ties may be weaker in the future – making family care, perhaps, less feasible. Since boomers have also had smaller families than previous generations, they are less likely to have an adequate support network: many are going to have to pay for the help they didn't give birth to. According to a 2001 survey of boomers commissioned by the GE Centre for Financial Learning in the US, 70 per cent of boomers do not even plan to rely on their family to take care of their long-term needs in their later years.[85]

In our interviews with baby boomers, the vast majority voiced a desire to maintain their independence for as long as possible, but struggled to come up with practical measures that would enable them to do so. Many began by imagining that friends and relatives would step into the breach and care for them, but they were also realistic enough to know that that might not happen.

> *I might not get it.*
>
> *We look after our parents and I look at the generation now and think 'will they look after us?'. I'm always asking myself that question and you can't get that answer.*

Most of our baby boomers were proud and vigorously independent, too proud to feel comfortable relying on their family and friends:

> *I don't want to feel like a silly old bugger, like I'm a pain.*
>
> *I think the thing is that nobody wants to be dependent on anybody else and people just want to be as self-sufficient as you can.*

For the vast majority, a central concern was to avoid being a burden to their children. Many admitted that caring for their parents was not a realistic option for themselves. Others had had experience of looking after their own parents or parents-in-law and admitted to finding this difficult. They wanted to avoid doing the same thing to their own children. The baby boomers may be loath to feel obliged to pass on their accumulated wealth, it seems, but the other side of this new social bargain is that they seem much happier to pay for care than to stifle the lives of unwilling children.

> *I wouldn't expect them to stop their lives to care for me.*
>
> *I'm inclined to think that we've had reasonably good lives, so I think it's time to let our children have their time and, you know, rather than be looking after us old, you know, decrepit people in wheelchairs. I'm not saying that they can't come to visit us, you know, once a week, or whatever, you know, to suit themselves sort of thing.*
>
> *I don't really expect anything of my kids, I would be grateful if it would happen but they have their own lives. I wouldn't expect them to stop their lives to look after me.*
>
> *To be honest I wouldn't want my parents living with me and it doesn't make me a very nice person.*

Even those who would look after their parents made it clear that it was not their obligation to do so, but a voluntary choice:

> *Yes, I mean I would do everything I possibly could for my mother. What I'm saying is she shouldn't expect it.*

A substantial minority actually preferred the idea that they could pay for services instead:

> *At the moment, I'd ask friends. But who knows in the future? Who could you turn to?*
>
> *I'd provide for that beforehand. I wouldn't want to depend on anyone.*

Some expressed the view they would not wish to see strangers performing intimate acts of care or seeing them physically/mentally debilitated.

> *I wouldn't like a stranger to have to come in and bathe me.*

For the most part, however, any lingering resentment on the part of our interviewees towards being looked after by strangers was based on a perception that current levels of care – either in-home, or in rest homes/sheltered accommodation – was either prohibitively expensive or very poorly delivered. For most of them, opting to be looked after by their children was a defensive rather than a positive choice and was often expressed with a great deal of guilt. Our baby boomers were extremely loath to be looked after by their children. They were simply unable to be convinced by the alternatives, or were deeply depressed at the level of care provided to many of the already old.

> *The horror is the old people's home where they all sit around in a big circle in front of the television. That is not what anyone wants, you have lost control then.*

Of all the groups interviewed, the Asian women expressed the least guilt about the prospect of being cared for by their children. Although they were anxious about whether this would happen, and didn't want to curtail their children's lives, the model of being looked after by their children was still considered an ideal. It was a pattern that they were used to, and which they felt was appropriate for the maintenance of family bonds.

Case study – Sustainable Trynwalden, the Netherlands

Trynwalden is a rural area in the north-east of Friesland in the Netherlands. With a population of about 9,000 spread across seven villages, the area used to represent a distinct community. Nevertheless, like many rural areas across Europe, it began to experience a population flight, the wasting away of infrastructure and a disintegration of the bonds of local community. Residents began to migrate to urban areas in search of the work and services that Trynwalden could no longer provide. Older people relocated to urban areas in search of better facilities.

Beginning in the mid-1990s, the Sustainable Trynwalden project has started to reverse this decline. A wide range of local organisations – including local authorities, a health insurance company, housing corporations, care and health institutions such as the hospital and the nursing home and older people themselves in the form of an advisory council of older people – helped develop the project. The initiative received additional funding through obtaining experimental status within the Dutch government programme of modernisation of long-term care. Financial independence, with few budgetary constraints and regulations, and experimental status enabled the project to take an entirely different approach and try out new and innovative working practices.

In Trynwalden there are as many different ways of providing services as there are older users. On a practical level the Sustainable Trynwalden initiative is described as a 'supermarket', in which the products of various service agencies are available to older people in the area. This focus on user needs has proven itself to cost as much as the previous system of service delivery. According to Foeke de Jong, Director of Sustainable Trynwalden: 'We have an under-consumption of care [compared with the national average] of 36.6 per cent. We think for the customers, on average, it is just a little bit more expensive. But the quality is much higher. For the government it's cheaper. Totally, for the council, the government, the taxes, and health insurance, it is a little, just a little more expensive.'

At the heart of the personalised services provided by Sustainable Trynwalden are the so-called 'Omtinkers', brokers in housing, welfare and care who assist older service users and their families in finding and accessing the right services to satisfy their needs and wishes. Trynwalden has four independent 'Omtinkers', each responsible for about 300 older adults. They function outside existing bureaucracies and can outflank or sideline them. After consultation with users, their role is to buy, using service vouchers, the most suitable service for the individual older person from Sustainable Trynwalden itself or any other organisation. They also ensure that users receive the services they have asked for and need, and pass on complaints and grievances. In other words, the 'Omtinkers' ensure that the voice of the service users is heard and responded to.

The second pillar of the initiative is the role of the so-called 'Doarpstallen', the five multidisciplinary teams – each consisting of home helps, home carers, nurses, social workers and, on call, a physiotherapist, ergotherapist, general practitioner, spiritual counsellor and priest – which jointly serve the seven villages. The crack troops of the 'Doarpstallen' offer all their services in the client's home during the day. Since the teams are self-organised and self-supporting, they have to fulfil a minimum of bureaucratic procedures. Care support is available around the clock. At night a two-person team is available for professional assistance answering alarm calls from anywhere in the region.

All the care homes in Trynwalden have been torn down. A newly built apartment building, with apartments equipped with the latest assistive technologies, offers accommodation to those older people who prefer to live in sheltered housing rather than at home. All apartments in the apartment building have been equipped with integrated and state-of-the-art computerised systems which provide increased safety (through fire, burglary and gas detection systems), comfort (through warmth and energy regulation), communication opportunities (through information, internet chatting, e-commerce) and care (through virtual or online access to care services).

A central service centre provides a variety of social services to older people and the wider community. It contains a GP and pharmacy, a dentist, a physiotherapy practice, a care hotel and day centre for older people, welfare and social counselling, a restaurant which offers assistance with eating, a library, a crèche, medical care facilities for children and a playground. In order to encourage communication between generations the service centre also includes a youth club for local young people. This youth centre also provides a convenient access point for potential volunteers from among the teenage population of Trynwalden.[86]

Rebranding home help

International research into the values of baby boomers suggests that they will want to stay in their homes for as long as possible, without the need to rely upon either children or strangers. Doubtless, the UK government will want to encourage the new generation of older people to do so, instead of supplying them with expensive long-term care.

Our research evidenced a great deal of nervousness among baby boomers about becoming less mobile and thus frail and dependent on others. Practised at being in control, it seems, the idealistic baby boomers find it difficult to accept that they might one day have to relinquish that control. 'The thing that terrifies me,' one baby boomer recently told the *Sydney Morning Herald*, 'is that in my dotage I become the captive of the nursing home and health system when I've always been in control of my life.'[87] Among our interviewees, the possibility of senility gave rise to a great deal of fear, as did the prospect of illness and protracted pain or suffering. People talked about becoming 'trapped' by their physical dependence on others. Perhaps unrealistically, our interviewees found the idea of being cared for as constraining and patronising. Faced with an idea for a video-link with support workers, for example, they scoffed at the suggestion that they might need 'somebody to check up on them'. Confronted with the idea of a once-a-day telephone call to ensure their good health, some were too proud to welcome such a service:

> *I would simply be too proud.*
>
> *I would resent some strange person just calling me every day to check that I'm okay.*
>
> *This does not apply to people with families.*

Another contradicted him:

> *You cannot assume that.*

Others were less proud, and more fearful:

> *You hear of people lying dead in their house for three days and no one has called on them or if they don't have good neighbours. And if you're on your own that will be the scenario and if someone's just going to phone every day, maybe two times a day, morning and evening, it only takes a second.*

The Stannah Stairlift was mentioned spontaneously in more than one group as a living symbol of old age which indicated that you were probably 'past it' – a fate that our interviewees wanted to avoid.

> *I never would have one of those put in. It's degrading. [People] sit there, like idiots, like they are sitting on the loo.*
>
> *I'd feel like a child in a pram.*
>
> *You lose all your dignity.*
>
> *I know some people need them but I would find that degrading.*

Our research suggests that the Stannah brand, if not the whole idea of stairlifts, is in slow decline in the imagination of baby boomers. But that, in turn, raises a series of thorny questions. Is this self-consciously youthful and idealistic generation simply being unrealistic in its expectations of old age? Will its expectations be rapidly brought down to earth when baby boomers realise that they are going to need a stairflift to get around? If baby boomers are going to turn up their noses at it when they reach old age, perhaps we need to think about building hundreds of thousands of 'age-proof' new homes which make the whole idea of stairlifts redundant? Lastly, we might think that the unpopularity of stairlifts is simply a matter of communication, and that Stannah (or another brand which is not so tarnished in the minds of baby boomers) can renew its offering by simply communicating with a new generation of its customers in a different way. 'If I were Stannah Stairlifts,' one of our expert interviewees told us, 'I would have someone a bit more interesting than a woman carrying a basket of knitting in the ads, and also have them doing something interesting and active as well as just being ferried up and down by the lift.'

Case study – the coming SMARTHOME

The majority of charities, academic research groups and commercial operations that design and develop assistive technology focus on meeting the needs of people with disabilities, advanced age-related conditions or learning difficulties. As a result, the most commonly cited examples of 'assistive technology' tend to be products such as chairlifts, wheelchairs and educational aids. There is, however, an expanding market for more subtle forms of assistive technology designed to cater for the less acute needs of baby boomers. These products fall into one of two categories – either labour-saving devices which aim to reduce the stress and strain of everyday activities, or products which attempt to compensate for the mild sensory degradation commonly experienced by baby boomers.

The idea of the purpose-built, technologically-advanced SMARTHOME has excited academics and futurologists for some years, and is a good example of an assistive technology which might be ideally suited to the material and aesthetic needs of baby boomers.[88] In the average prototypical SMARTHOME, for example, small motors and sensors are fitted to moveable objects around the house and are operated by a single infrared controller. Doors, windows and curtains can be automatically opened to varying degrees; sinks and cupboards, mounted on lifting mechanisms, can be raised to optimally accessible heights; baths and sinks can be filled to particular levels and at specific temperatures; lights can be turned on and off from a distance.[89]

In the SMARTHOME, sophisticated technology can take the hard work out of household maintenance. Take the Robomower,[90] an automatic lawnmower that cuts grass, mulches it up into power and leaves the remains on the lawn as a natural fertiliser. Or the Electromelt system,[91] a network of heating cables which melts snow and ice on driveways. High-tech services can be supplemented by more basic devices to ease the undertaking of household activities and chores. BT, for example, already provides large-button telephones with louder volume controls. It offers to print phone bills and phone books in large fonts with wide spacing, a boon for baby boomers who are coping with failing eyesight.[92] Household maintenance can be eased by providing long-handled sponges, brooms, dustpans and dusters, large-print tape measures and T-handled screwdrivers. Having thereby effortlessly completed the day's household chores, our baby boomer might retire to a whirlpool 'deepheat' bath, specifically designed for older individuals suffering from muscle stiffness and arthritis.[93]

There was also a great deal of irritation at the kind of language which routinely conflates old age and disability. A case study about future-proof homes, for example, was widely disliked as patronising and laden with negative associations.

This sounds like a disability thing.

That is not just for old people is it, it is for disabled people. It doesn't strike me as being for old people, it is for someone with a disability.

But neither did they seem very enthusiastic about the future housing that they would be offered:

We are all going to be living in little boxes.

Some felt that the only solution would be to build new housing. Their concerns about new housing were mainly about demographic exclusion. A minority of baby boomers were quite happy to consider living in communities which are exclusively designed for older people, but many others expected this to be stultifying and boring and preferred mixed developments. Clearly, the answer is for choice and flexibility in the construction of such developments.

It is going to have to be a completely new development, like the new towns.

This will pose positive planning challenges for local authorities charged with the delivery of new large public housing developments and towns where the conventional understanding of 'mixed use' has had more to do with domestic/commercial sharing than the needs of mixed generations.

Some Australian boomers have decided how this might look for them: an updated version of communal living, relying more on friends pooling resources and living together:

A wheel with spokes . . . a central area – maybe a studio, kitchen, library – with walkways to our private houses.

This model also offers interesting inter-generational options: the separate, private quarters are planned to accommodate ongoing family lives and the diversity of life experiences of baby boomers where some have young children and some have grandchildren; and to ensure that core members of the 'commune' won't have to live in the same space with someone's grown child returned home after the divorce.

These boomers felt that 'the arrangement is better than being in a nursing home where you might not get on with 80 per cent of the people'.[94]

In the United States, where the friends-helping-friends model for ageing is more advanced, arrangements akin to prenuptial agreements are under consideration.

Paul Kleyman, editor of *Ageing Today*, told the *New York Times*, 'Before long, there'll be a business to help people do this.'[95]

ICT and care

The UK is one of only two European countries to give explicit mention to the use of new information and communication technologies (ICT) in its policy-making documents about the care of older people.[96] This has manifested itself in a series of interesting pilots which aim to do two things: first, to use so-called 'assistive technology' to make care for older people more efficient and less intrusive, and second, to make information about the range of care options available more accessible. The government's CARE direct initiative is a good example of a 'one-stop shop' gateway to information and help about a whole range of services available to older adults including social care, health, housing and social security benefits. A series of six local authority pilots have been run successfully in the South West.[97]

Several more pilots of innovative schemes bringing information and communication technologies to today's elderly are already under way. Microsoft UK, for example, has recently teamed up with Age Concern and Citizens Online, to launch a pilot initiative. Among other things, the scheme will help support the establishment of an Age Concern mini-explorer bus, a roving IT training facility offering Mobile Internet Taster Sessions (MITS) taking IT to older people who are socially and geographically isolated.[98] Nevertheless, the fluency of today's baby boomers with the new technologies will undoubtedly throw up new and more ambitious schemes to enhance processes of elder care and to assist boomers to retain their cherished independence.

But there are dangers. Confronted with the idea for an interactive telephone service which offered a video-link with a support worker, many felt that such technology is 'taking over' and is cutting out real human interaction; for many this was a frightening picture of a cold and inhuman future. The danger, however, is that the increased use of assistive technologies may only exacerbate the alienation felt by the new old, who may end up swapping the attentions of a carer for an unsatisfactory relationship with an electronic device.

I think there is also danger of relying too much on technology that you can isolate all human contact.

The rise of the 'seasoned single'

As the baby boomers begin their slow march towards retirement, one of the most obvious changes in the demographic structure of all advanced industrialised countries will be, with increasing rates of divorce and rising numbers of people remaining unmarried, more and more baby boomers living on their own at a younger age. A report published in the UK in March 2001 by research agency Consumer Futures forecast that middle-aged single people will account for more than 40 per cent of a 4 million-strong rise in household numbers over the next 20 years.[99]

This is the cohort which is already being identified by marketers as the 'seasoned singles'. Nowadays, senior citizens who live alone are more likely to be widowed than divorced. About one-third of all women over the age of 55 are widowed, according to the latest figures from the US Current Population Survey, while just 15 per cent are either divorced, separated or never married in the first place. But the same set of figures also indicates that nearly 16 per cent of boomers aged 35–44 have never married compared with just 6 per cent of 35–44-year-olds in 1970. Even boomers who have married at some point in their lives are far more likely to be divorced by the time of retirement. The survey also finds that baby boomers of all ages make up nearly 60 per cent of all divorced people over the age of 15 in the

United States, although they account for just 40 per cent of the population aged 15 and older.

Those statistics, according to the AARP, mean that the current wave of baby boomers in the US is far more likely to end up living alone than previous generations of seniors. This trend also applies in the UK. It is forecast that '41 per cent of the 1940s cohort [1946–50] will be living alone by age 75 compared with 38 per cent of the 1930s cohort [1931–5] and 37 per cent of the 1916–1920 cohort. Furthermore, a quarter (26 per cent) of the 1960s cohort will already be lone householders by age 60.' This makes it 'likely that close to half of the 1960s [1961–5] boomers will be living solo by age 75'.[100]

The emergence of the seasoned single, together with the preference of baby boomers to receive home care for as long as possible, may mean that they will need to rely more on private services which were previously available without charge from their spouses. This is something, as we have already seen, which will come easier to consumer-savvy baby boomers than it would have done for previous generations. 'There's been hesitation among today's older adults about relying on private services,' says Karen A Roberto, director of the Center for Gerontology at Virginia Tech in the US. 'But the boomer generation,' she adds, 'has grown up with purchasing services as a way of life – as an example, they purchased day care for their children. That trend will carry over into later life.'[101]

Hell is other baby boomers

While the vision of single living was attractive to many of our interviewees, many also voiced concern about being lonely and about losing touch with their friends and relatives. An important concern for our baby boomer interviewees was being excluded from everyone apart from those in their own immediate age cohort. Asked to inhabit a planet populated solely by baby boomers, for example, the universal reaction among our interviewees was to baulk at the prospect:

I would hate it.

I would miss my kids and grandchildren.

It would be very quiet.

It would be like an asylum.

There would be nothing to talk about.

I would be bored stiff.

I think we would be killing each other.

More generally, many seemed convinced that governments in other countries were more respectful of the needs of the elderly.

This government have got to look after the old people, number one priority. I have been to other countries like France and Belgium and they really look after the old people.

There is more loyalty over there [Ireland]. Free TV, free travel. They have done their bit for their country and they are treated and respected as senior citizens, they are well looked after.

Indeed, some expressed preference for what they described as a 'continental' model in which the extended family live in close proximity to each other, where grandparents still have a vital role to play in supporting and being involved with younger generations.

You can't segregate the young from the old.

What would they prefer instead, we asked?

More interactivity with people, not being excluded from the community.

I would hope to become part of the community and I think that's really, really important especially in old age, you know, and you hear of people who have been dead in their flat for three weeks.

A sense of community spirit.

We like to socialise, at tea-dances and clubs. Nobody wants to be locked in their houses.

Remaining part of the community is important. Being able to receive guests and carry on as best you can.

There is good evidence that the baby boomers are going to be formidable political articulators of their own interests and to press their demands for better provision from government. But what struck us about British baby boomers was their lack of interest in being part of a social club of people their own age. What they feared most of all was being marginalised or excluded. Perhaps because of their fetish for youth or because they feared being marginalised as older people, our interviewees could not think of anything worse that being surrounded only by other baby boomers.

Absolutely horrendous.

Nothing good.

It will be wall-to-wall arguments.

There would be no innovation, there would be nothing new.

Herein lies a much more general lesson, which might apply equally well to government as to those in the marketing and communication industries: baby boomers do need to be targeted as a cohort, but it is potentially dangerous to target them overtly or to single them out as a social group.

Support and the ethnic dimension

We already know that the boomers will be a more ethnically diverse generation than their parents and this will present new challenges in providing formal and informal care for older people. According to Harper and Levin of the Oxford Institute of Ageing,[102] the care of the elderly within minority ethnic communities is still a hugely under-researched area and much still remains unknown. They do, however, question the widely held assumption that minority ethnic communities will 'look after their own'. That assumption is dangerous and inaccurate, and could, for three main reasons, lead to inequities within the boomer generation along ethnic lines. In the first place, the boomer generation is more diverse than earlier cohorts because of significant immigration to the UK since the 1950s and 1960s. Families then may be split and unable to provide care for their elders because of migration itself.

> *There [in Jamaica] you have all your extended family. Everybody relies on each other.*

Secondly, Harper and Levin stress that living within an extended family is not the same as ensuring an adequate level of care for the elderly. An extended family, they argue, may be a form of 'containment' rather than good care. Close-knit families can be sources of intrusiveness, bad advice and conflict as well as support.

Finally, where communities such as the large Asian one in Britain do have strong traditions of filial responsibility and care, these important norms may be threatened by the boomers' children who have become more Westernised or have 'married out' of the ethnic community. Harper and Levin cite a study undertaken in Camden, North London, where elders see the joint Bangladeshi and Islamic heritage as being eroded by the influences of British culture. They fear their children have become, or are becoming, Westernised and as a consequence are developing the 'uncaring and individualistic' attitudes of English people towards older people.

Our research among minority ethnic baby boomers showed a degree of nervousness among these groups about what arrangements might be made for their care in the future. Whereas patterns within their culture meant that many of our minority ethnic interviewees (and especially Asian women) were duty-bound to look after their parents in old age, and to live in an extended family context, they were keenly aware that their own children were less likely to feel the same obligations towards them as they had felt towards their own parents. This left many of them (again, particularly the Asian women) worrying about who would care for them when they were older. While they hoped that their children would want to look after them, they also wanted to avoid becoming a burden on their children, or preventing their children making a success of themselves. Many appeared torn between the traditional values that they had been brought up to respect and the new ways of life that they could see their children adopting.

I think things will be different by the time I'm in my 60s . . . and these children will be totally different from the way I am. They're not going to be like me, when I get back from work and I'm running around taking my mum shopping because that is what is done in our culture.

Unlike many of our white baby boomers, who mourned the collapse of traditional values and communities, many of those in our minority ethnic groups voiced pride in the support and neighbourliness which they still felt was very strong within their communities. For these groups, continuing to share activities with others of the same ethnic group was a high priority, eg sharing home-cooked meals. And even those who had admitted to themselves that they would be forced to look outside their family for help were adamant that any care would be best provided by those within their own ethnic group.

I think they are better, more sensitive to your needs.

The best ones are old black ladies, more sensitive to your needs, who come to look after another black lady.

Only a Pakistani person would know what type of food a Pakistani person would eat.

7. Ethics, equity and fair trading

The stereotypical image of the baby boomers is of a generation that rebelled against the establishment and existing social order by taking to the streets, and which produced the founders of a range of social and political movements, from the feminist to the environmentalist to the civil rights movement. But how true is the stereotype, and how far will baby boomers put their money where their mouth is when it comes to grafting ethics on to their purchasing decisions?

Our initial research suggested that baby boomers are pioneering ethical consumers. Twenty-three per cent of baby boomers have boycotted a company's product on ethical grounds, compared with only 13 per cent of the older generation and 16 per cent of the younger generation. Equally, 20 per cent of boomers have positively chosen to buy a product or service because of the company's ethical reputation.[103] And our baby boomer interviewees liked nothing more than to rage against the greed of big businesses and multinationals.

> *They are a con, so that is why I want to do away with designer labels, I want quality goods but I do not want somebody telling me they are just because they are made by Gucci.*

> *You just look around and I see shops just full of rubbish and we are stripping the earth of all its resources and the population is increasing . . . Things like that do worry me and I try to do what I can to a certain extent.*

I think it is the big corporations and manufacturing companies that are going to have to be lobbied by the government to make changes.

There is too much greed.

Yes, it's unethical to shop at Tesco now because they're making 4.5 million a day.

In addition, many displayed a kind of 'anything goes' tolerance on social issues.

I think our generation are much more liberal, I think they're much more open to new ideas.

The preference of baby boomers for introducing ethics into their purchasing decisions is also illustrated by their dislike of brand names and their choice of travel destinations. In the UK, for example, a survey suggests that baby boomers are the generation which least trusts brand names such as Ford, Coca-Cola, Nike and Barclays.[104] Given their instinctive hostility towards multinationals and their cynicism about branding, there is good evidence that the baby boomers might be the real No Logo generation:

Our research suggests that Naomi Klein may be the last baby boomer, rather than the voice of radical youth. No Logo *was very digestible for baby boomer corporate types. But young people, we find, are much more fickle, much more happy to collude with brands. They are also much less impassioned about politics. It does seem that the baby boomers are doing most of the politicised shouting. They also imply that their agenda is shared by the next generation, whereas the evidence suggests that it is not.*

Tamar Kasriel, The Henley Centre

But whatever their aspirations, our research among British baby boomers found scant evidence that they were prepared to put their money where their mouth is. Awareness of 'ethical consumption' or 'ethical trading' was very low across the groups. A minority of our interviewees claimed that they were doing their bit:

> *You do a little recycling. You help out a little bit.*
>
> *Buying fair trade products . . . it sounds a bit corny but you have to give a bit back, don't you really.*

The majority, however, appeared disillusioned by politics, or by the possibilities of collective action.

> *If we voted with our feet and boycotted things, we could change – we could change what the supermarkets sell in them. And we have the power to do that. But we don't collectively do it. Because Tesco's are terrible for the way they treat their suppliers.*
>
> *I have no idea, I would like to see it addressed, yes but there are such huge problems I guess, it is very difficult to see how we can make a difference.*
>
> *I don't think it's down to the individual, it has got to be down to a government body.*
>
> *You try to recycle things and all that but I have got a life to live as well and I don't make myself a martyr to all this sort of thing.*

Many were left feeling guilty about what they considered to be the selfishness of their generation:

> *I mean if it is a fair trade one or a good quality other one, and they are normally more expensive, aren't they? I will go for it if it is not much more, but if it is a lot more, if I am being honest I will not.*
>
> *I think we are a greedy, selfish generation basically and I think*

most of us would like to buy ethically, to live our lives ethically, but when it comes down to it, we would like to live within our budgets and our budgets constrain us more than we would like.

I'm sure I'm selfish. I like cars, so I saw a nice big Mercedes there, and I thought well, I'd like a nice Mercedes.

At the end of the day you have got to look after number one.

Certainly, most of them believed that environmental awareness, for example, would become a more important issue in the future. But in the meantime, they felt that it was up to government to take action rather than individuals. Even if the boomers do weigh the state of the world rather heavily, their disillusionment with political activism and their acute sensitivity to price leaves them reluctant to change their purchasing decisions accordingly. It may be that our interviewees simply had a sophisticated understanding that real social change could not be effected by simply changing their purchasing decisions.

For a minority, the idea of environmental awareness came up against the boomers' stubborn individualism: environmental initiatives were seen by a number of our interviewees as an affront to personal liberty, as the unwarranted interference of 'officialdom' in how they chose to live their lives. A vocal minority were concerned by the authoritarian implications of all these restrictions:

Being encouraged to recycle is okay. But being dictated to is beyond the pale. You should not interfere with other people's rights.

Government can bully you.

Ethical issues seemed to be matters of grave concern for our interviewees only when they were combined with issues of quality, usability or personal safety. When asked about the environment, many were suspicious that there was something going wrong with the climate. Spontaneously, for example, many of our groups raised fears about GM foods. Even here, however, their enthusiasm for making the switch to organic came up against the barrier of price.

I would like to [choose organic] but I am not doing it. I like to buy organic free range chicken because that is what I would rather put my money into but then again sometimes I don't.

A lot of these things are so much more expensive and people haven't always got the choice.

The ethical and environmental concerns of our interviewees might translate into action only when they join forces with their concerns about design and usability. In a recent poll of 2,000 Britons over 50, for example, 99 per cent thought packaging had become harder to open in the last ten years. A full 71 per cent of respondents to the survey said that they had been injured as they struggled to open food packaging, and 97 per cent thought there was just 'too much excess packaging'.[105]

Equity and intra-generational relations

As a demographic group, baby boomers are currently the most wealthy and powerful cohort in British society. They have, for example, the highest average income and expenditure in the population.[106] They also own more assets: they are, for example, the largest group of owner-occupiers in Britain.[107]

For significant numbers of baby boomers this current wealth will continue into old age and will enable them to afford a comfortable retirement. But amid all the hype about boomers' wealth, it is often forgotten that there will be many boomers in lower socioeconomic groups who will most certainly face financial problems – the 20 per cent of baby boomers who, as the recent government pension green paper points out, have no private pension and plan to rely entirely on state provision.[108]

The instinctive radicalism of baby boomers, however, does not seem to extend to the transfer of their wealth to disadvantaged baby boomers. The majority of our baby boomer interviewees, for example, seemed resigned to the increasing privatisation of public services and the entrenchment of a two-tier system:

> *Money talks.*
>
> *The people who can afford it will go and get what they want.*
>
> *I am going to be joining PPP. Not because I don't believe in the NHS, because I really do, I'm really pro-NHS. But I really think they've got so many constraints and they're so burdened and underfunded that really you've got to do something for yourself if you can afford to do a bit yourself because otherwise you're not going to be seen. I think the waiting list is your biggest concern.*
>
> *I think over the next 20 years we will see a huge burden on the health service, whether it will go private, something has got to happen. Within the next 20 years we will see that difference, whether it is to our benefit as an individual, I do not know, but something has got to happen with that. We cannot keep pumping in the billions that they are and really not achieving anything.*

Current wealth divisions within the baby boomer generation are likely to become more pointed as the cohort continues to age. This may mean, for example, that while one segment of the baby boomer generation will be able to afford the holidays and customised products described in previous chapters, others may struggle to find their basic living expenses. Once again, however, our baby boomers felt little social solidarity as a generation.

> *I think we are all selfish and think of number one, so at the end of the day the only people I want to help, I will help my own kids, so yes I am selfish, I am not going to help anyone else.*
>
> *[Redistributing wealth through a generation] sounds like income tax to me and I do not like that much.*

It was hardly surprising that our interviewees from lower-income groups – facing concerns about their financial security – tended to see fewer possibilities available to them for the future. For these middle-aged people, old age was more likely to be viewed with fear and apprehension than as a unique chance for exploration or the learning of new things. Many of them were looking forward to retirement as a chance to put their feet up after years of hard work, often in manual or low-paid jobs, or after years of bringing up children. By contrast, our interviewees at the higher end of the income spectrum were more likely to see older age as an opportunity to try new things, to fulfil long-dormant hopes and aspirations and to get involved in the world around them in entirely new ways.

Extremes of wealth within the baby boomer generation raises important questions about the potential role of service providers to bridge wealth inequalities among the ageing baby boomer generation. Many public and voluntary service providers are already committed to balancing intra-generational wealth inequalities and their consequences. Thus, for instance, the NHS, with its continuing ethos of free treatment at the point of delivery, is committed to treating effectively the health problems that occur as a result of poverty, and ensuring that all baby boomers from all socioeconomic groups have equal access to health service provision.

That ethos is more difficult to find among private service providers, whose service provision is driven by market demands rather than a commitment to social justice. All of which raises two questions. Will ageing baby boomers demand services from the private sector which serve the needs of all baby boomers and bridge intra-generational inequalities? If this is not the case, and the individualistic attitudes of baby boomers suggests that it will not be, will future governments see a role for themselves in promoting intra-generational equity by encouraging private sector service providers to balance inequalities? For instance, will the government encourage or even require private sector providers in receipt of public funds to balance inequalities through some new form of community service obligation?

Conclusion

The current British Prime Minister and the President of the United States are both baby boomers. It is worth remembering that baby boomers cannot be characterised as some beleaguered and disenfranchised minority in need of empowering. Taken as a demographic group, they are the wealthiest cohort in contemporary society, healthier than any previous generation of middle-aged people and more than capable of looking after themselves. As this unusually weighty demographic cohort begins its long march towards retirement, our research suggests that its approach to growing old is likely to be profoundly different.

Take retirement. Governments are already actively looking for ways to persuade people to work for longer. Our research suggests that the postwar idea of retirement, in which people were compulsorily fenced off from the rest of society and paid to do nothing, has now reached the end of its natural life. As they look forward to old age, today's baby boomers do not want to be forced to work until they drop. But they also refuse to see their lives as broken up into linear stages – education, work, parenthood – with retirement the end of the line and the reward. Instead, they increasingly prefer to see their life as a never-ending cycle, one which enables them to seamlessly dip in and out of periods of education, work and leisure.

If social institutions want to keep up, there is little time to lose. Harnessing the creativity and the productivity of the new old is not at all a matter of altruism. As a demographic group, baby boomers are not only wealthy but are predisposed to spend their money on goods and services which make their lives and the lives of those around them easier. As consumers, they want to be treated as individuals. They want, wherever possible, the opportunity to customise not only products but also a highly sophisticated web of support services.

But baby boomers are valuable not only as well-heeled consumers but as productive and experienced workers. As the supply of ready labour in advanced industrial societies dwindles, organisations in the public, private and voluntary sectors will find themselves in a race to win the loyalty of older people. A government which wants to benefit from the creativity and continued labour of its ageing population needs to ensure that baby boomers who want to dip in and out of periods of work, education and travel are not mired in bureaucracy for their efforts. Employers will need to place as much of a premium on experience as they currently place on the vigour of youth. Voluntary organisations can think about how to stimulate a new generation of volunteers to action.

Harnessing the energy and interest of the baby boomers also means supporting them in lifestyles which prolong independence, wellness, self-reliance and social sustainability, all things which will reduce pressure on our systems of health and social care. But channelling their time, expertise, creativity and credibility into social and public institutions will be equally important.

If there is a blind spot on the radar of baby boomers, our research suggests, it is when they come to think about the inevitability of old age. It is a cruel irony that our ageing society is hampered by such trepidation about the natural process of ageing. 'With full-span lives having become the norm,' wrote the essayist Ronald Blythe back in 1922, 'people may need to learn how to be aged as they had once had to learn how to be adult.'[109] If baby boomers are to be fully at ease with the ageing process, they need to be more accepting of the process of growing old. In order to challenge the prevailing gloom about ageing, we need urgently to invent a collective story about the value of growing older. Organisations that can assist in framing that story are likely to find a powerful and positive response.

Notes

1 Figures from the Datamonitor report 'Senior Consumers', 30 April 2002. For more information on the report, see www.datamonitor.com/~ba010c0666424ac58d8b4a4b917f2b28~/consumer/reports/product_summary.asp?pid=DMCM0088.

2 From the report *Ageism: too costly to ignore* (Employers Forum on Age (EFA), 2001); see: www.efa.org.uk/pressreleases/press.asp?articleid=10&cid=6&num=.

3 J Huber and P Skidmore. *The New Old: why the baby boomers won't be pensioned off* (London: Demos, 2003).

4 M Carrigan and I Szmigin. 'Advertising in an ageing society', *Ageing and Society* 20 no 2 (2000): 217–33.

5 For more on this, see A Giddens, *Beyond Left and Right* (Cambridge: Polity, 1994).

6 UK Government green paper, *Simplicity, Security and Choice* (2002); available at: www.dwp.gov.uk/consultations/consult/2002/pensions/#summary.

7 J Leland, 'Boomers' secret smokes up the closet', *New York Times*, 14 July 2002.

8 H Nicholson, 'French revolution', *The Times*, 24 Sept 2002.

9 BR Levy, MD Slade, SR Kunkel and SV Kasl, 'Longevity increased by positive self-perceptions of aging', *Journal of Personality and Social Psychology* 83 (2002): 261–70.

10 F Schirrmacher, *Das Methusalem Komplott*, (Muenchen: Blessing, 2004).

11 J Queenan, 'I don't do grief', *The American Spectator*, May 2001.

12 RW McChesney and JB Foster, 'The commercial tidal wave', *Monthly Review*, March 2003.

13 MORI, Social Research Institute, 2002; D Hughes, 'The march of the Meldrews; middle-aged, grumpy and gunning for Blair', *Daily Mail*, 27 Aug 2002.

14 D Wanless, *Securing our Future Health: taking a long-term view*, (London: HSMO, 2002).

15 L Singhania, 'Boomers changing the way charities do business', *Associated Press*, 10 Sept 2002.

16 Commonwealth Department of Health and Aged Care, *Population Ageing and the Economy* (Commonwealth of Australia, 2001); see: www.ageing.health.gov.au/ofoa/documents/pdf/popageing.pdf.
17 'The demand for anti-ageing products is set to rise by around 11% per year', *Cosmetics International*, 12 Sept 2003.
18 MJ Weiss, 'Chasing youth', *American Demographics*, Oct 2002.
19 Figures from the New York research company Packaged Facts, *Australian Financial Review*, 22 June 2003.
20 'Faith Popcorn with 2003 trends', *ABC News Transcripts*, 1 Jan 2003; 'Trends to live by? Primal passions expected to steal limelight next year', *Chattanooga Times/Chattanooga Free Press*, 29 Dec 2002.
21 Weiss, 'Chasing youth'.
22 Ibid.
23 Survey conducted for 'Living TV', *Press Association*, 15 Jan 2004.
24 Study published by BUPA, *Irish News*, 28 Jan 2004.
25 J Harkin, 'Brand on the run', *Independent on Sunday*, 2 Mar 2003.
26 J Strausbaugh, *Rock Till You Drop* (London: Verso, 2001).
27 'Older collectors give Hornby a future', *Guardian*, 12 June 2002.
28 P Sims, 'Grandparents "worth £1bn a year" in gifts', *Press Association*, 26 Sept 2002.
29 The idea of an 'experience economy' was first articulated by business thinker James H Gilmore. See JH Gilmore, 'Welcome to the experience economy', *Harvard Business Review*, July/Aug 1998.
30 W Berry, 'For baby boomers, education is youth', *Newsday*, 18 Aug 2002; P Danziger, *Why People Buy Things They Don't Need* (Ithaca, NY: Paramount Market Publishing, 2002).
31 'Older travellers booming', *Sunday Times (Australia)*, 4 Apr 2004.
32 K Hoggan, 'Sea change hits the cruise industry', *Calgary Sun*, 17 Nov 2002.
33 K Scott and P Barkham, 'Cruises head for a sea change in clientele', *Guardian*, 19 May 2004.
34 S Theil, 'Marketing the elder set', *Newsweek*, 16 Sept 2002.
35 K Vann, 'Size matters to advertisers pitching to boomers', *Edmonton Journal*, 9 Aug 2002.
36 J Demers, 'Grey power', *CMA Management* 76, no 5 (July/Aug 2002): 14.
37 Study based on an interview with Lorian Coutts, Director of Communications, B&Q (30 April 2004). See also B&Q's website, www.diy.com and R Brown, *Inclusive Design Guidelines – towards usable products for everyone* (London: Kingfisher and B&Q, June 2004).
38 G Malkani, 'Affluent over-50s accuse advertising industry of ignoring the "grey pound"', *Financial Times*, 26 Apr 2004.
39 For more on preferences and the values which underlie them from an economic perspective, see, for example, C Sunstein, *Free Markets and Social Justice* (Oxford: Oxford University Press, 1997).
40 'OAPs' spending spree', *The Times*, 18 Feb 2004.
41 B Lippert, 'The right stuff; Sony defies stereotypes, with over-50s just as cool (and snarky) as the kids', *ADWEEK*, 2 Dec 2002.

42 'Homeowners: sons and daughters', a survey of parents who are owner-occupiers, was carried out for the Joseph Rowntree Foundation by the MORI Social Research Institute, published 17 June 2004.
43 To view a summary of the Datamonitor report, see www.datamonitor.co.uk/~26a50c6eae05441688cd6b59c5d8e3c3~/financial/Reports/product_summary.asp?pid=DMFS1491.
44 'Blair admits being Darkness fan', *BBC News Online*, 14 Nov 2003.
45 T de Lisle, 'Melody maker', *Guardian*, 1 Mar 2004.
46 In 2002, for example, women bought 41% of all albums, up from 38% the year before. *Sunday Express*, 14 Mar 2004.
47 E Gardner, 'Evolution of pop', *USA Today*, 12 Mar 2004.
48 'Some companies toning down sexy ads', *United Press International*, 16 Apr 2004.
49 'An aging generation of baby boomers,' opined one commentator, 'is increasingly queasy about the often-grungy sexual imagery that has become almost second nature to kids.' *USA Today*, 16 Apr 2004.
50 C Ayres, 'US advertisers compete for the grey dollar', *The Times*, 9 Apr 2004.
51 MORI, *Trust in Public Institutions* (London: MORI, 2003).
52 Office for National Statistics, *Labour Force Survey* (London: ONS, 2000).
53 Interview with Tamar Kasriel, Associate Director, The Henley Centre, 2 Feb 2004.
54 See www.segundajuventud.org/spanish/.
55 MORI, *Nestle Family Monitor – lifelong learning and volunteering* (London: MORI, 2000).
56 Study based on an interview with Susan Snyder, Director, Senior Wellness Project (23 April 2004). For more information, see www.seniorservices.org.
57 J Maxmin and S Zuboff, *The Support Economy: why corporations are failing individuals and the next stage of capitalism* (London: Allen Lane, 2003).
58 J King, 'Changing social trends are set to present water companies with an even greater opportunity to market home services', *Utility Week*, 13 Dec 2002; D Kaplan, 'Ad recovery in sight', *ADWEEK*, 25 Nov 2002.
59 Study based on interviews with Louise Parkes, Head of Corporate and Events Fundraising, Help the Aged (7 May 2004) and Lucy Shadbolt, Senior Marketing Manager, British Gas (16 April 2004).
60 B Rayner, 'Finding the right name for over-50 boomers', *Richmond Times Dispatch (Virginia)*, 9 Feb 2004. The survey was carried out by Boisseau, an advertising agency based in Richmond, VA, USA.
61 '"It's Hip to H.E.A.R.™" program helps educate a generation in denial about hearing loss', *PR Newswire*, 5 May 2004.
62 D O'Briant, 'Advertisers discovering 50-plus', *The Atlanta Journal and Constitution*, 31 Dec 2002.
63 e-MORI Technology Tracker, April 2004.
64 MORI, *Social Values* (London: MORI, 1999).
65 Acxiom Precision Marketing website, 4 July 2004, www.claritas.co.uk/uk/news/press_releases/1110201?version=1.

66 Claritas Consumer Research UK, 2003, ibid.
67 See: www.microsoft.com/enable/products.
68 See: www.apple.com/accessibility/.
69 See: www.hp.com/hpinfo/abouthp/accessibility.
70 See: www.adapt-it.org.uk.
71 Y Kageyama, 'Boomer marketing still testing new ground in youth-worshipping in Japan', *Associated Press Worldstream*, 12 Aug 2002.
72 See: www.abledata.com.
73 Ibid.
74 Brown, *Inclusive Design Guidelines.*
75 Study based on an interview with Michelle Sohn, Senior Product Manager, OXO International, 6 May 2004. For more information, see OXO International, www.oxo.com.
76 J Harkin and P Skidmore, *Grown-Up Trust* (London: Demos, 2003).
77 MORI, *Trust in Public Institutions.*
78 'Could a pill prevent grey hair?', *BBC News Online*, 27 May 2004.
79 A Mooney and J Statham, *The Pivot Generation: informal care and work after fifty* (Bristol: Policy Press, 2002).
80 S Nuttall, RJL Blackwood, BMH Bussell et al, *Financing Long-term Care in Britain* (London: Institute of Actuaries, 1993).
81 F McGlone and N Cronin, *A Crisis in Care: the future of family and state care for older people in the European Union* (Occasional Paper 19) (London: Family Studies Policy Centre, 1994).
82 Interview with George Leeson, Oxford Institute of Ageing (11 Feb 2004).
83 S Harper and S Levin, *Changing Families as Societies Age: care, independence and ethnicity*, Working Paper number WP503 (Oxford: Oxford Institute of Ageing, University of Oxford, 2003).
84 J Bornat, B Dimmock and S Peace, *The Impact of Family Change on Older People: the case of stepfamilies* (Essex: ESRC, 2003).
85 'The next big singles market, baby boomers retire the idea of marriage in their golden years', *Forecast*, 20 Aug 2001.
86 Study based on an interview with Foeke de Jong, Director, Sustainable Trynwalden, 15 April 2004; see www.skewiel-trynwalden.nl.
87 A Horin, 'A retreat back to communes', *Sydney Morning Herald*, 6 Mar 2004.
88 See: www.abledata.com.
89 See: www.jrf.org.uk/housingandcare/smarthomes/devices.asp.
90 See: www.friendlyrobotics.com.
91 See: www.abledata.com.
92 For more information see www.btplc.com/age_disability/index.htm.
93 See: www.abledata.com.
94 Horin, 'A retreat back to communes'.
95 'Older women team up to face future together', *New York Times*, 27 Feb 2004.
96 Belgium is the other country. RG Curry, M Trejo Tinoco and D Wardle, *The Use of Information Communication Technology (ICT) to Support Independent Living for Older and Disabled People* (London: The Department of Health, 2002).

97 See: www.caredirect.gov.uk/about.htm.
98 A Coleman, 'Training; IT comes of age for older surfers', *Express*, 10 Feb 2004.
99 'Singles set to soar', *Retail Week*, 2 March 2001.
100 M Evandrou and J Falkingham, 'Looking back to look forward: lessons from four birth cohorts in the 21st century', *Populations Trends* 99, no 101 (October 2000): 11–18.
101 'The next big singles market'.
102 Harper and Levin, *Changing Families as Societies Age.*
103 MORI survey on corporate social responsibility (2002).
104 'Age emerged as the most important factor in explaining difference – with the young being the least likely to hold anti corporate views.' Quotation from Michael Willmott, and based on research commissioned by The Future Foundation in the UK. For more information, see M Willmott, *Citizen Brands: putting society at the heart of your business* (Chichester: John Wiley and Sons, 2001).
105 '"Wrap rage" hitting the over-50s', *BBC NewsOnline*, 4 Feb 2004.
106 ONS, *New Earning Survey* (London: Office for National Statistics, 2001).
107 *Family Resource Survey Great Britain 1999–2000* (London: Office for National Statistics).
108 UK Government green paper, *Simplicity, Security and Choice.*
109 R Blythe, *The View in Winter: reflections on old age* (London: Allen Lane, 1979).

DEMOS – Licence to Publish

THE WORK (AS DEFINED BELOW) IS PROVIDED UNDER THE TERMS OF THIS LICENCE ("LICENCE"). THE WORK IS PROTECTED BY COPYRIGHT AND/OR OTHER APPLICABLE LAW. ANY USE OF THE WORK OTHER THAN AS AUTHORIZED UNDER THIS LICENCE IS PROHIBITED. BY EXERCISING ANY RIGHTS TO THE WORK PROVIDED HERE, YOU ACCEPT AND AGREE TO BE BOUND BY THE TERMS OF THIS LICENCE. DEMOS GRANTS YOU THE RIGHTS CONTAINED HERE IN CONSIDERATION OF YOUR ACCEPTANCE OF SUCH TERMS AND CONDITIONS.

1. **Definitions**
   - **a** **"Collective Work"** means a work, such as a periodical issue, anthology or encyclopedia, in which the Work in its entirety in unmodified form, along with a number of other contributions, constituting separate and independent works in themselves, are assembled into a collective whole. A work that constitutes a Collective Work will not be considered a Derivative Work (as defined below) for the purposes of this Licence.
   - **b** **"Derivative Work"** means a work based upon the Work or upon the Work and other pre-existing works, such as a musical arrangement, dramatization, fictionalization, motion picture version, sound recording, art reproduction, abridgment, condensation, or any other form in which the Work may be recast, transformed, or adapted, except that a work that constitutes a Collective Work or a translation from English into another language will not be considered a Derivative Work for the purpose of this Licence.
   - **c** **"Licensor"** means the individual or entity that offers the Work under the terms of this Licence.
   - **d** **"Original Author"** means the individual or entity who created the Work.
   - **e** **"Work"** means the copyrightable work of authorship offered under the terms of this Licence.
   - **f** **"You"** means an individual or entity exercising rights under this Licence who has not previously violated the terms of this Licence with respect to the Work, or who has received express permission from DEMOS to exercise rights under this Licence despite a previous violation.
2. **Fair Use Rights.** Nothing in this licence is intended to reduce, limit, or restrict any rights arising from fair use, first sale or other limitations on the exclusive rights of the copyright owner under copyright law or other applicable laws.
3. **Licence Grant.** Subject to the terms and conditions of this Licence, Licensor hereby grants You a worldwide, royalty-free, non-exclusive, perpetual (for the duration of the applicable copyright) licence to exercise the rights in the Work as stated below:
   - **a** to reproduce the Work, to incorporate the Work into one or more Collective Works, and to reproduce the Work as incorporated in the Collective Works;
   - **b** to distribute copies or phonorecords of, display publicly, perform publicly, and perform publicly by means of a digital audio transmission the Work including as incorporated in Collective Works;

   The above rights may be exercised in all media and formats whether now known or hereafter devised. The above rights include the right to make such modifications as are technically necessary to exercise the rights in other media and formats. All rights not expressly granted by Licensor are hereby reserved.
4. **Restrictions.** The licence granted in Section 3 above is expressly made subject to and limited by the following restrictions:
   - **a** You may distribute, publicly display, publicly perform, or publicly digitally perform the Work only under the terms of this Licence, and You must include a copy of, or the Uniform Resource Identifier for, this Licence with every copy or phonorecord of the Work You distribute, publicly display, publicly perform, or publicly digitally perform. You may not offer or impose any terms on the Work that alter or restrict the terms of this Licence or the recipients' exercise of the rights granted hereunder. You may not sublicence the Work. You must keep intact all notices that refer to this Licence and to the disclaimer of warranties. You may not distribute, publicly display, publicly perform, or publicly digitally perform the Work with any technological measures that control access or use of the Work in a manner inconsistent with the terms of this Licence Agreement. The above applies to the Work as incorporated in a Collective Work, but this does not require the Collective Work apart from the Work itself to be made subject to the terms of this Licence. If You create a Collective Work, upon notice from any Licencor You must, to the extent practicable, remove from the Collective Work any reference to such Licensor or the Original Author, as requested.
   - **b** You may not exercise any of the rights granted to You in Section 3 above in any manner that is primarily intended for or directed toward commercial advantage or private monetary

compensation. The exchange of the Work for other copyrighted works by means of digital file-sharing or otherwise shall not be considered to be intended for or directed toward commercial advantage or private monetary compensation, provided there is no payment of any monetary compensation in connection with the exchange of copyrighted works.

c If you distribute, publicly display, publicly perform, or publicly digitally perform the Work or any Collective Works, You must keep intact all copyright notices for the Work and give the Original Author credit reasonable to the medium or means You are utilizing by conveying the name (or pseudonym if applicable) of the Original Author if supplied; the title of the Work if supplied. Such credit may be implemented in any reasonable manner; provided, however, that in the case of a Collective Work, at a minimum such credit will appear where any other comparable authorship credit appears and in a manner at least as prominent as such other comparable authorship credit.

5. Representations, Warranties and Disclaimer

a By offering the Work for public release under this Licence, Licensor represents and warrants that, to the best of Licensor's knowledge after reasonable inquiry:

i Licensor has secured all rights in the Work necessary to grant the licence rights hereunder and to permit the lawful exercise of the rights granted hereunder without You having any obligation to pay any royalties, compulsory licence fees, residuals or any other payments;

ii The Work does not infringe the copyright, trademark, publicity rights, common law rights or any other right of any third party or constitute defamation, invasion of privacy or other tortious injury to any third party.

b EXCEPT AS EXPRESSLY STATED IN THIS LICENCE OR OTHERWISE AGREED IN WRITING OR REQUIRED BY APPLICABLE LAW, THE WORK IS LICENCED ON AN "AS IS" BASIS, WITHOUT WARRANTIES OF ANY KIND, EITHER EXPRESS OR IMPLIED INCLUDING, WITHOUT LIMITATION, ANY WARRANTIES REGARDING THE CONTENTS OR ACCURACY OF THE WORK.

6. Limitation on Liability. EXCEPT TO THE EXTENT REQUIRED BY APPLICABLE LAW, AND EXCEPT FOR DAMAGES ARISING FROM LIABILITY TO A THIRD PARTY RESULTING FROM BREACH OF THE WARRANTIES IN SECTION 5, IN NO EVENT WILL LICENSOR BE LIABLE TO YOU ON ANY LEGAL THEORY FOR ANY SPECIAL, INCIDENTAL, CONSEQUENTIAL, PUNITIVE OR EXEMPLARY DAMAGES ARISING OUT OF THIS LICENCE OR THE USE OF THE WORK, EVEN IF LICENSOR HAS BEEN ADVISED OF THE POSSIBILITY OF SUCH DAMAGES.

7. Termination

a This Licence and the rights granted hereunder will terminate automatically upon any breach by You of the terms of this Licence. Individuals or entities who have received Collective Works from You under this Licence, however, will not have their licences terminated provided such individuals or entities remain in full compliance with those licences. Sections 1, 2, 5, 6, 7, and 8 will survive any termination of this Licence.

b Subject to the above terms and conditions, the licence granted here is perpetual (for the duration of the applicable copyright in the Work). Notwithstanding the above, Licensor reserves the right to release the Work under different licence terms or to stop distributing the Work at any time; provided, however that any such election will not serve to withdraw this Licence (or any other licence that has been, or is required to be, granted under the terms of this Licence), and this Licence will continue in full force and effect unless terminated as stated above.

8. Miscellaneous

a Each time You distribute or publicly digitally perform the Work or a Collective Work, DEMOS offers to the recipient a licence to the Work on the same terms and conditions as the licence granted to You under this Licence.

b If any provision of this Licence is invalid or unenforceable under applicable law, it shall not affect the validity or enforceability of the remainder of the terms of this Licence, and without further action by the parties to this agreement, such provision shall be reformed to the minimum extent necessary to make such provision valid and enforceable.

c No term or provision of this Licence shall be deemed waived and no breach consented to unless such waiver or consent shall be in writing and signed by the party to be charged with such waiver or consent.

d This Licence constitutes the entire agreement between the parties with respect to the Work licensed here. There are no understandings, agreements or representations with respect to the Work not specified here. Licensor shall not be bound by any additional provisions that may appear in any communication from You. This Licence may not be modified without the mutual written agreement of DEMOS and You.